Donn Byrne Intermediate
Comprehension
Passages

with Recall Exercises and Aural
Comprehension Tests

Longman

PEARSON EDUCATION LIMITED
Edinburgh Gate, Harlow
Essex CM20 2JE, England
and Associated Companies throughout the World

www.longman.com

First published 1964
Fifty-seventh impression 2005

ISBN 0 – 582 – 52386 – 9

Printed in Malaysia, PP

Contents

Introduction

This book provides material for reading and listening comprehension and can be used in the year preceding the Cambridge First Certificate (or any other comparable) examination. The texts, although written with the needs of students at this level in mind, are not graded, so that throughout, the learners are being exposed to natural language. The book is divided into three related sections:

Section One This consists of thirty texts, with exercises for oral and written work. The following points should be noted:

Exercise 1   Multiple choice type questions, phased out as the book progresses.

Exercise 2   Wh- type questions, increased as the book progresses.

Exercise 3*   (Passages 1–20 only) Yes/No type questions.

Exercise 4*   Completion type exercises, which involve restatement (and therefore interpretation) of part of the text.

Exercise 5   Vocabulary exercises (multiple choice in the early stages.)

Exercise 6   Guided composition exercises, which involve re-presentation of part of the text, usually from a personal angle.

Exercise 7   Practice in some point of usage in the text.

Section Two This consists of Recall Exercises. These are extracts from the texts in Section One, with certain grammatical features omitted or incomplete. The extracts are arranged in four groups; tenses, articles, prepositions and adverbial particles, and linking words. References for each extract are provided; they can therefore be corrected by the students themselves and are thus suitable for self-access work.

Section Three This consists of two types of exercise. First, aural comprehension passages. These passages are based, linguistically and thematically, on texts in Section One, as indicated by the references in brackets at the end of each passage. These passages can also be used for 'reproduction' work; that is, the passage is read aloud and the students reproduce the ideas in their own words. Secondly, there are twelve dictation passages, which are similarly based on material in Section One.

---

* Since Exercise 3 is discontinued after Passage 20, Exercise 4 becomes Exercise 3 (and so on.)

How to use this material

The following approach is suggested:

1 Use one of the reading goals (provided at the end of the book) to get the students to do a quick first reading of the text.

2 Read the text aloud to the class and/or get them to read it again silently. If the students are reading silently, use either Exercise 1 or 3 as a reading incentive.

3 Discuss any points of interest (e.g. what the text is about.) Since the texts are mostly narrative, it is a good idea at this stage to get them to supply some background (e.g. for the people, places and other events mentioned in the story.) In short, try to bring the text alive as much as possible. Here or later the students may like to suggest a title for the text.

4 Do the text-related exercises 1–5. The students may work individually, in pairs or in groups. These exercises follow a set pattern, as indicated in the Introduction.

You may wish to do alternative or additional exercises in connection with the text. The following are some possibilities. All references are to the first text:

a Are the following statements true or false? If they are false, give the correct statement.

For example: The writer was driving the car.

This is false – the writer's companion, John, was driving.

b Give more details.

For example: We had little food with us.

They only had a few biscuits and some chocolate.

c Explain why.

For example: John went for a walk.

He was a poor sleeper.

d What do you think they said?

For example: I asked John to drive more slowly.

'Will you please drive more slowly ... Hey! Not so fast!'

5 Get the students to react to the text. For this type of largely narrative text, there are two main ways in which this can be done:
   a Ask the students to suggest a continuation to the story where this is appropriate. Another possibility is to ask them to decide on a hypothetical turn of events (e.g. What would have happened if they had both gone to sleep?) The students may also be asked to say what they would have done in the circumstances.
   b Ask the students to relate any similar experience they have had.
6 Exercises 6 and 7 may be done at any convenient point. Exercise 6 is particularly suitable for homework. In the early stages, some class preparation will usually be necessary to show the students how to extract relevant ideas and how to re-present these in a properly sequenced form. It is not necessary to insist on the word limit suggested in the exercise, especially if there is any risk of inhibiting the students from using linking words. Note that the 'continuation' activity, suggested in 5 above, can also be done as a writing activity.
7 The exercises in Section Two are best done about a week after the other activities.
8 Follow the usual procedure for reading aloud the listening comprehension and dictation passages.

Comprehension Passages   I

It was already late when we set out for the next town, which according to the map was about fifteen miles away on the other side of the hills. There we felt sure that we would find a bed for the night. Darkness fell soon after we left the village, but luckily we met no
5 one as we drove swiftly along the narrow winding road that led to the hills. As we climbed higher, it became colder and rain began to fall, making it difficult at times to see the road. I asked John, my companion, to drive more slowly.

After we had travelled for about twenty miles, there was still
10 no sign of the town which was marked on the map. We were beginning to get worried. Then, without warning, the car stopped. A quick examination showed that we had run out of petrol. Although we had little food with us, only a few biscuits and some chocolate, we decided to spend the night in the car.
15 Our meal was soon over. I tried to go to sleep at once, but John, who was a poor sleeper, got out of the car after a few minutes and went for a walk up the hill. Soon he came running back. From the top of the hill he had seen, in the valley below, the lights of the town we were looking for. We at once unloaded all our luggage
20 and, with a great effort, managed to push the car to the top of the hill. Then we went back for the luggage, loaded the car again and set off down the hill. In less than a quarter of an hour we were in the town, where we found a hotel quite easily.

1 *Choose the best answer.*
  a The travellers had a map but
    (i) they did not know how to use it
    (ii) it gave them the wrong information
    (iii) they could not see it very well in the dark
    (iv) the town they were looking for was not clearly marked
  b Their car stopped because
    (i) they had travelled more than twenty miles
    (ii) the petrol ran out of it
    (iii) there was no petrol left
    (iv) they were going uphill

2 *Answer the following questions briefly, in your own words as far as possible. Use one complete sentence for each answer.*
  a What did the travellers expect to find in the next town?
  b How long did it take them to reach the town after they set off down the hill?

3 *Answer these questions, using only short form answers.*
  a Was it dark when they left the village?
  b Did they push the car up the hill easily?

4 *Complete the following sentences. Your answers must be related to the ideas contained in the passage.*
  a The writer asked John to drive more slowly because ......
  b John went for a walk because ......
  c "......", said John, after he had run back to the car.
  d ...... so that it would be easier to push it to the top of the hill.
  e They would have spent the night in the car if ......

5 *Choose the best explanation according to the context.*
  a winding (5) means
     (i) going uphill   (ii) dangerous
     (iii) not straight   (iv) cold
  b without warning (11) means
     (i) suddenly   (ii) nobody told them
     (iii) before it got hot   (iv) without any explanation

6 *Composition* Imagine that you were John. Describe in not more than 90 words what you did from the time you got out of the car until you reached the town. Do not include any ideas which are not in the passage. Use your own words as far as possible.

7 *Notice this sentence:*
    They *managed to* push the car to the top of the hill.
  Manage(d) to + infinitive is a common way of describing achievement, something successfully done, often in spite of difficulties.

  Now rewrite these sentences, replacing the verbs in italics by *managed to* + infinitive.

  a My hat fell into the river, but I *succeeded in getting* it *out*.
  b In the end, after a long argument, we *were able to persuade* them.
  c He *succeeded in passing* his driving test, although he was a bad driver.
  d *Were* you *able to find* the book you wanted?
  e How on earth *did* you *succeed in finding out* where I live?
  f They *were able to put* the fire *out* before the house burnt down.
  g No prisoner *has* ever *succeeded in escaping* from here.
  h If I'd *been able to get* some sleep, I shouldn't have felt so tired the next morning.
  i I can't understand how he *was able to keep* awake.
  j He made a good excuse, but he *didn't* quite *succeed in convincing* me.

2

While I was walking along the road the other day I happened to notice a small brown leather purse lying on the pavement. I picked it up and opened it to see if I could find out the owner's name. There was nothing inside it except some small change and a rather
5 old photograph—a picture of a woman and a young girl about twelve years old, who looked like the woman's daughter. I put the photograph back and took the purse to the police station, where I handed it to the sergeant in charge. Before I left, the sergeant made a note of my name and address in case the owner of the purse wanted to
10 write and thank me.

That evening I went to have dinner with an uncle and aunt of mine. They had also invited another person, a young woman, so that there would be four people at table. The young woman's face was familiar, but I could not remember where I had seen it. I was
15 quite sure that we had not met before. In the course of conversation, however, the young woman happened to remark that she had lost her purse that afternoon. I at once remembered where I had seen her face. She was the young girl in the photograph, although she was now much older. Of course she was very surprised when I was
20 able to describe her purse to her. Then I explained that I had recognised her face from the photograph I had found in the purse. My uncle insisted on going round to the police station immediately to claim the purse. As the police sergeant handed it over, he said that it was a remarkable coincidence that I had found not only the
25 purse but also the person who had lost it.

1 *Choose the best answer.*

   a The purse which the writer found
    (i) was empty
    (ii) had some money in it
    (iii) had a few coins and a photograph in it
    (iv) had an old photograph in it

   b The writer recognised the young woman because
    (i) he had met her somewhere before
    (ii) she was the woman in the photograph
    (iii) she often had dinner with his uncle and aunt
    (iv) she looked rather like the young girl in the photograph

2 *Answer the following questions briefly, in your own words as far as possible. Use one complete sentence for each answer.*
  a Why did the sergeant make a note of the writer's name and address?
  b Where did they go to get the purse back?

3 *Answer these questions, using only short form answers.*
  a Did the writer find the owner's name in the purse?
  b Was the young woman surprised when the writer described her purse?

4 *Complete the following sentences. Your answers must be related to the ideas contained in the passage.*

  a When the writer opened the purse, he hoped ......
  b The sergeant had a book, in which ......
  c The young woman ...... so that there would be four people at table.
  d The writer said: "There was a photograph in the purse. That is how ......"
  e "Let's ......," the writer's uncle insisted.

5 *Choose the best explanation according to the context.*
  a *familiar* (14) means
(i) common	(ii) known
(iii) famous	(iv) domestic

  b *claim* (23) means
(i) pretend	(ii) identify
(iii) ask for	(iv) take

6 *Composition* Imagine that you were the young woman in the story. Describe in not more than 90 words what happened from the time you went to the house for dinner until you got your purse back at the police station. Do not include any ideas which are not in the passage. Use your own words as far as possible.

7 *Notice this sentence:*
    The young woman *happened to remark* that she had lost her purse. This means: She *remarked, quite by chance,* that she had lost her purse. Similarly: I *happened to notice* ...... means I *noticed, quite by chance,* ......

4

Now rewrite these sentences, replacing the verb in italics by *happen to* + infinitive.

a I was just coming out of the station when I *saw* an old friend.
b Mary *said* she liked flowers, so George sent her some.
c I didn't hear the news until I *got* a letter from John.
d That pen you found *is* mine.
e He didn't see the beginning of the film because he *arrived* late.
f We wanted to go for a walk this afternoon, but it *rained*.
g If you *see* Mary, tell her to ring me up.
h Do you *know* where Peter has gone?
i I'd like to lend you the money, but I *haven't got* any.
j The tree fell right across the road, but luckily no one *was passing* at the time.

3

There are five people at our table, including myself. I've already
learnt a great deal about them in the short time we have been at sea,
although we rarely meet except at meal-times.

First of all, there is Dr Stone—my favourite, I must confess. He
5 is a man of about sixty-five, with grey hair and a humorous face.
He gave up his practice a short while ago and is now travelling
round the world before he retires to some quiet country village. As
a young man, he served abroad for many years as a doctor in the
Army. He speaks several languages and has told us a great deal
10 about the ports we are going to call at. He seems to have been
everywhere. During the day, when he is not talking to his fellow
passengers (one gets the impression that he already knows everybody on board!), he sits on deck reading or else gazes out to sea
through an old-fashioned telescope.

15 Then there is "grandmother". I call her that because her name
escapes me. In spite of being a grandmother, she looks remarkably
young, not more than forty-five. She is on her way to visit a daughter
who emigrated to Australia some years ago. Naturally she is very
excited at the thought of seeing her again, and her three grand-
20 children, whom she has never seen. She can talk of little else.
This voyage is a great adventure for her: she has never been abroad
before.

Then there is a man I do not care for very much, an engineer
by the name of Barlow. He has been on leave in England and is
25 now returning to his work in Singapore. He seems full of
energy: he swims or plays tennis the best part of the day. I have
never in my life met a man with such a loud laugh. He has the
cabin next to mine and I can hear his laugh even through the
wall!

The other person who sits at our table is Mrs Hunt. I have
30 found out hardly anything about her. She is extremely quiet
and rarely talks, except to consult the doctor about her
children's various ailments. She is on her way to join her husband
in India.

* Extract from a diary.

1 *Choose the best answer.*
  a Dr Stone is travelling round the world because
     (i) he likes meeting a lot of people
     (ii) he is having a holiday before he retires
     (iii) he wants to visit the places he knew in the past
     (iv) he enjoys travelling abroad
  b The writer calls the second person at the table "grandmother" because
     (i) she looks old
     (ii) she has three grandchildren
     (iii) he has not been told her name
     (iv) he has forgotten her name

2 *Answer the following questions briefly, in your own words as far as possible. Use one complete sentence for each answer.*
  a How does Dr Stone spend his time when he is not talking to his fellow passengers?
  b Why is "grandmother" going to Australia?

3 *Answer these questions, using only short form answers.*
  a Does the writer spend a lot of time with the people who eat at his table?
  b Is "grandmother" the oldest person at table?

4 *Complete the following sentences. Your answers must be related to the ideas contained in the passage.*

  a Dr Stone ...... after he has travelled round the world.
  b Dr Stone seems to know everyone on board because ......
  c Barlow spends most of his time ......
  d Barlow has such a loud laugh that ......
  e The writer does not know much about Mrs Hunt because ......

5 *Choose the best explanation according to the context.*
  a *remarkably* (16) means
     (i) attractively   (ii) quite
     (iii) noticeably   (iv) extraordinarily
  b *on leave* (24) means
     (i) about to go   (ii) away from work
     (iii) absent   (iv) at home

7

6 *Composition* Write an imaginary description, in about 75 words, of the writer of this passage. Make it read like an extract from a diary of your own.

7 *Notice these sentences:*

We *rarely* meet except at meal-times.

I can *never* remember her name.

She has *never* been abroad before.

Frequency adverbs (i.e. those which answer the question "How often?") are most commonly placed in front of the *principal* verb in the sentence. Here are examples in interrogative and negative sentences:

Does it *often* rain in June?

He didn't *always* finish his breakfast.

Common adverbs of this kind are: *always, never, often, seldom, usually, generally, sometimes.*

Adverbial phrases such as *every day (week,* etc.), *once (twice,* etc.) *a day (month,* etc.) are normally placed at the end of the sentence:

He buys a newspaper *every morning.*

She has to see the doctor *twice a week.*

Now complete the following sentences by putting the adverb or adverbial phrase in its correct position in the sentence.

a I arrive home later when I travel by bus (*usually*).

b Does John stay out late (*often*)?

c The postman brings the letters at eight o'clock (*every morning*).

d Our letters are sent by airmail (*seldom*).

e He writes to his parents (*twice a week*).

f She doesn't look unhappy (*generally*).

g Whenever I'm busy, I forget the time (*always*).

h Who is the man who sits next to you on the bus (*sometimes*)?

i He worked hard when he was a young man (*never*).

j Do you drink a lot of water in hot weather (*usually*)?

4

Half an hour before daybreak three of the boys assembled, as they
agreed, near the old bridge. The fourth, a boy by the name of
Tolly, had not turned up. His absence did not greatly surprise the
others. They knew that his mother did not want him to come on
5 this expedition into the forest.

Charles, who was the oldest and their accepted leader, waded
downstream to the place where their boat was tied up in the shelter
of some overhanging bushes. Then he rowed the boat back to the
shallow water near the bridge, where the boys loaded it with the
10 provisions, blankets and other things which they were taking on
their journey.

Dawn was just breaking as they climbed into their boat and
pushed off from the bank. A swift current carried them downstream, so there was no need to row. They took it in turns to keep
15 the boat in the centre of the river. Three hours later they entered
the forest where they intended to spend the next few days.

"Let's go ashore now and make some tea," suggested Charles.
"No one will see us here."

It was forbidden to light fires in the forest, but people rarely
20 came this way.

While Charles tied the boat up, the other two boys set about
gathering wood for a fire. When they came back, each with a large
handful of sticks, they found Charles looking very worried.

"We haven't got any matches," he announced gloomily. "Tolly
25 was going to bring them."

This was bad news. They were miles away now from the nearest
shop.

1 *Choose the best answer.*

  a The boys did not have to row because
    (i) they had plenty of time to get to the forest
    (ii) they kept their boat in the centre of the river
    (iii) the river carried their boat along quite quickly
    (iv) they had pushed off from the bank

  b The boys could not light a fire because
    (i) the wood was too big
    (ii) Charles had forgotten to bring any matches

(iii) it was forbidden to light fires in the forest
(iv) the boy who was going to bring the matches had not come on
the expedition

2 *Answer the following questions briefly, in your own words as far as
possible. Use one complete sentence for each answer.*
a How long did it take them to load the boat?
b When did Charles discover that they had no matches?

3 *Answer these questions, using only short form answers.*
a Was it light when they set off downstream?
b Did Charles also go to gather wood?

4 *Complete the following sentences. Your answers must be related to the
ideas contained in the passage.*

a The name of the boy who ...... was Tolly.
b It was easier to load the boat near the bridge because ......
c The boys did not have to row because there was ...... which ......
d While they were going downstream, all the boys had to do
was ......
e Although ......, the boys went ashore to make tea.

5 *Choose the best explanation according to the context.*
a *waded* (6) means
    (i) crossed the river   (ii) swam
    (iii) went out of sight   (iv) walked slowly through the water
b *in turns* (14) means
    (i) round and round   (ii) one after the other
    (iii) all together   (iv) from time to time

6 *Composition* Imagine that you were Charles. Describe in not more
than 90 words what you did from the time you waded downstream
to fetch the boat until you discovered that you had no matches.
Do not include any ideas which are not in the passage. Use your
own words as far as possible.

7 *Notice this sentence:*
The other two boys *set about gathering* wood for a fire.
In this pattern the verb is followed by a gerund. Here are two more
examples:
Would you *mind speaking* more quietly?

10

The children *enjoyed playing* in the park.

Now complete the following sentences by choosing a suitable verb from the list given at the foot of the exercise.

a Let's go for a walk as soon as it stops ......
b They kept on ...... a noise even after I asked them to stop.
c Mary never minds ...... the dinner.
d She begged her husband to give up ...... his pipe in bed.
e I don't remember ...... you a Christmas card this year.
f Grandfather enjoys ...... television.
g Fancy ...... an overcoat on a hot summer's day!
h I couldn't help ...... what you said about me.
i Why on earth did you suggest ...... the car red?
j Have you ever considered ...... abroad to work?

cook	paint	smoke
go	rain	watch
hear	send	wear
make		

11

5

The children stopped chattering as Miss Hughes entered the classroom. Then they stood up as one body and said in a loud chorus:

"Good morning, teacher."

Miss Hughes smiled, said good morning too and told the class
5 to sit down. At a glance there seemed to be about thirty-five pupils in the class. The majority were girls. She noticed several intelligent faces. All the pupils were watching her intently, waiting no doubt to find out what sort of person she was.

"I suppose you want to know my name," she said. But before she
10 could tell them, someone in the class called out, "It's Miss Hughes." Everybody laughed. Miss Hughes laughed too.

"News travels quickly," she said. "I'm afraid it will take me longer to learn all your names."

Miss Hughes opened the attendance register and called their
15 names in turn. When she came to the last name on the list, John Young, she noticed that he had been absent for over a month.

"What's the matter with John Young?" she asked, looking up.

"He's in hospital, Miss Hughes," said a fair-haired girl in the front row. "He's broken his leg."

20 "He slipped on the ice," added one of the boys.

"Has anyone been to see him in hospital?" Miss Hughes asked. No one replied.

It was time to start the lesson. "Now let me see," said Miss Hughes, looking at the timetable. "The first lesson is English."

25 "Oh! please tell us a story," begged one of the girls.

Several of the pupils repeated this. Miss Hughes smiled.

"Very well," she said. "But first of all I want you to write a letter to John Young. We'll send the best ones to cheer him up in hospital. Afterwards I'll tell you a story, if you're good."

30 They were all writing busily when Miss Hughes slipped out of the classroom to fetch a book which she had left in the staffroom. She passed the headmistress in the corridor.

"Any trouble from that class?" the headmistress asked.

"Not so far," said Miss Hughes confidently. "They all seem
35 very well behaved."

1 *Choose the best answer.*
  a Miss Hughes came into the classroom
     (i) but nobody took any notice of her
     (ii) and all the children stood up at the same time and said good
          morning
     (iii) and all the children said good morning
     (iv) and all the children stood up one after the other
  b Miss Hughes
     (i) refused to tell the class a story
     (ii) had forgotten her story book, so she asked the class to write
          a letter
     (iii) asked the class to write a letter before she told them a story
     (iv) asked the class to write a letter so that she could go to the
          staffroom

2 *Answer the following questions briefly, in your own words as far as
  possible. Use one complete sentence for each answer.*
  a Why did Miss Hughes say: "News travels quickly"?
  b What did Miss Hughes do in order to find out which pupils were
     present?

3 *Answer these questions, using only short form answers.*
  a Was Miss Hughes a new teacher?
  b Did Miss Hughes have any trouble from the class?

4 *Complete the following sentences. Your answers must be related to the
  ideas contained in the passage.*
  a "Good morning." Miss Hughes said to the class "......"
  b No one replied when Miss Hughes asked whether ......
  c Miss Hughes looked at the timetable in order to find out ......
  d Miss Hughes said that she wanted the class to write to John
     Young before ......
  e Miss Hughes met the headmistress while ......

5 *Choose the best explanation according to the context.*
  a *intently* (7) means
     (i) with a great deal of attention   (ii) by chance
     (iii) on purpose   (iv) unpleasantly
  b *not so far* (34) means
     (i) very near   (ii) very much
     (iii) to a small degree   (iv) not until now

6 *Composition*   Imagine that you were Miss Hughes. Describe in not more than 90 words what you did from the time you opened the register to call the names until you went out of the classroom. Do not include any ideas which are not in the passage. Use your own words as far as possible.

7 *Notice this sentence:*
   She noticed that he *had been* absent for nearly a month.
The Past Perfect tense is commonly used to show that one event or action in the past occurred before another event or action also in the past. Here is another example:
   . . . to fetch a book which she *had left* in the staffroom.
Notice that the Present Perfect becomes Past Perfect in Indirect Speech after a reporting verb in the Past tense.
   Miss Hughes asked whether anyone *had been* to see John Young.
The Past Perfect is used in the *if*-clause of this type of Conditional sentence.
   I would have helped you if you *had asked* me.

Now complete the following sentences by putting the verbs in brackets into the Past Perfect tense.

a He went to the police station with a purse that he ...... (*find*) on the pavement.
b Helen admitted that she ...... (*not, read*) *Hamlet*.
c By the end of the year they ...... (*save*) two hundred pounds.
d Miss Hughes would have gone back to the class at once if she ...... (*hear*) any noise.
e They wrote to say that they ...... already ...... (*buy*) a house.
f If there ...... (*be*) a mistake, I would have told you.
g I went to see my friend, who ...... just ...... (*come back*) from abroad.
h By the time Bill reached the shop, he ...... (*forgot*) what he was going to buy.
i How long did it take you to realise that you ...... (*see*) the film already?
j She would have missed her train if the bus ...... (*be*) late.

6

Bill Fuller, the postman, whistled cheerfully as he pushed his bicycle up the hill towards old Mrs Dunley's house. His work for the day was almost finished; his bag, usually quite heavy when he set out on his round, was empty now except for the letter that he had to deliver to Mrs Dunley. She lived over a mile from the village so that, when Bill had a letter for her, he always finished his day's work much later. He did not mind this, however, because she never failed to ask him in for a cup of tea.

When Bill entered the gate of Mrs Dunley's house, he was surprised not to find her working in her garden. She usually spent most afternoons there when the weather was fine. Bill went straight round to the back of the house, thinking that she might be in the kitchen. The door was locked and the curtains were drawn. Puzzled, he returned to the front of the house and knocked hard on the door. There was no answer. Bill thought that this was very strange because he knew that Mrs Dunley rarely left the house.

Just then he noticed that her bottle of milk, which was delivered early in the morning, was still on the doorstep. This worried him. If Mrs Dunley had not taken in her milk, perhaps she was ill. Bill walked round the house until he found an open window. It was small, but he just managed to squeeze through. He went into the hall. There he almost fell over Mrs Dunley, who was lying at the foot of the stairs, unconscious. Realising that there was little he could do for her, Bill rushed out of the house, stopped a passing car and told the driver to telephone for an ambulance as soon as he got to the village.

1 *Choose the best answer.*
  a Bill Fuller was going to Mrs Dunley's house because
    (i) she had asked him for a cup of tea
    (ii) he had some letters to deliver to her
    (iii) his day's work was over
    (iv) he had a letter for her
  b The thing that especially worried Bill was
    (i) finding the back door locked and the curtains drawn
    (ii) seeing her bottle of milk on the doorstep
    (iii) not getting any answer when he knocked on the door
    (iv) not finding Mrs Dunley in the garden

15

2 *Answer the following questions briefly, in your own words as far as possible. Use one complete sentence for each answer.*
   a How did Bill get into the house?
   b How did Bill get help for Mrs Dunley?

3 *Answer these questions, using only short form answers.*
   a Was Bill riding his bicycle up the hill?
   b Was Mrs Dunley alive when Bill found her?

4 *Complete the following sentences. Your answers must be related to the ideas contained in the passage.*

   a Bill's bag was not heavy because ......
   b When the weather was fine, Mrs Dunley ......
   c Bill was worried when he saw that ......
   d It was lucky that one of the windows was open, otherwise ......
   e As soon as Bill got into the house, he ......, where he found Mrs Dunley ......

5 *Choose the best explanation according to the context.*
   a *did not mind* (7) means
      (i) looked forward to   (ii) enjoyed
      (iii) did not remember   (iv) did not object to
   b *straight* (11) means
      (i) without going back   (ii) immediately
      (iii) fairly quickly   (iv) in a direct line

6 *Composition* Imagine that you were Bill Fuller, the postman. Describe in not more than 100 words what you did from the time you reached the gate of Mrs Dunley's house until you stopped the motorist. Do not include any ideas which are not in the passage. Use your own words as far as possible.

7 *Notice this sentence:*
   His bag, usually *quite heavy* when he set out ......
   The meaning of *quite* here is *moderately*: i.e. his bag was not excessively heavy, but it was not light either. In this sense *quite* is often close in meaning to *fairly* or *rather*, depending on the context. Compare this use of *quite* with the way it is used in Exercise 6 on page 85.

Now complete the following sentences by choosing a suitable

word or phrase from the list given at the foot of the exercise. Pay particular attention to the different ways in which *quite* is used.

a The restaurant was quite ......, but we managed to find a table near the door.

b According to the radio, it is quite ...... to rain tomorrow.

c There were quite ...... people at the meeting. Over a hundred, in fact.

d I'm feeling tired. I'd quite ...... to go to bed early tonight.

e The water is shallow here, but near the bridge it is quite ......

f They go to the theatre quite ...... At least once a fortnight.

g It was quite an ...... lecture, but I enjoyed the one yesterday more.

h I shall be sorry to leave this house. I've grown quite ...... it.

i Your daughter *has* grown up. She's quite ...... now!

j I can't remember exactly when we went there, but I know that it was quite ......

a long time ago	deep	like
a lot of	fond of	likely
a young lady	interesting	often
crowded		

7

Helen packed a small suitcase, said goodbye to her mother and hurried out of the house to catch the bus to the station. There was no one else waiting at the bus stop, so it looked as if a bus had just left. Helen looked at her watch anxiously: it was already two
5 o'clock. Her train left at two-thirty, and since it would take at least twenty minutes to reach the station, she did not have much time to spare, even if a bus came along at once.

Just then a taxi came slowly down the road. Helen knew that the fare to the station was at least two pounds, which was more
10 than she could afford; but she quickly made up her mind that it would be well worth the extra expense in order to be sure of catching her train. So she stopped the taxi and got in. She told the driver that she had to catch a train which left at half past two. The man nodded and said that he would take a short cut to get her to the
15 station in good time.

All went well until, just as they were coming out of a side-street into the main road that led to the station, the taxi ran into a car. There was a loud crash and Helen was thrown forward so violently that she hit her head on the front seat. Both drivers got out and
20 began shouting at each other. Helen got out as well, to ask them to stop quarrelling, but neither of them took any notice of her at all.

Helen was now quite sure that she was going to miss her train, although she was not very far from the station. She was wondering what to do when a bus came into sight, going in the direction of the
25 station. The bus stop was not far off, so Helen got her suitcase out of the taxi and ran towards the bus, which had stopped to let some passengers get off. The bus conductor saw her running and did not ring the bell for the bus to start until she had got on. Helen reached the station just in time and managed to catch her train after
30 all. But if she had waited for the taxi driver to stop arguing, she would probably have missed it.

1 *Choose the best answer.*
  a Helen took a taxi because
      (i) she was afraid of missing her train
      (ii) she did not want to wait for the bus
      (iii) it was already two o'clock
      (iv) she had a suitcase to carry

b In the end Helen
   (i) finished the journey by taxi
   (ii) did not reach the station
   (iii) did the last part of the journey by bus
   (iv) had to walk part of the way to the station

2 *Answer the following questions briefly, in your own words as far as possible. Use one complete sentence for each answer.*
   a Why did Helen think that she had just missed a bus?
   b What happened to Helen when the taxi ran into the car?

3 *Answer these questions, using only short form answers.*
   a Did Helen know how much it cost to go to the station by taxi?
   b Did Helen stop to pay the taxi driver?

4 *Complete the following sentences. Your answers must be related to the ideas contained in the passage.*
   a The train which Helen ...... left at two-thirty.
   b Helen did not usually go to the station by taxi because ......
   c The taxi driver nodded and said: "......"
   d The bus had stopped so that ......
   e If the bus conductor had rung the bell, Helen ......

5 *Choose the best explanation according to the context.*
   a short cut (14) means
      (i) interruption   (ii) quick way
      (iii) secret path   (iv) back street
   b as well (20) means
      (i) equally good   (ii) quickly
      (iii) feeling better   (iv) also

6 *Composition* Imagine that you were Helen. Describe in not more than 100 words what you did from the time the taxi came down the road until you caught the bus. Do not include any ideas which are not in the passage. Use your own words as far as possible.

7 In the passage there are several examples of the *to*-infinitive used to express purpose.
   Helen got out *to ask* them to stop.
   In order may be placed in front of the *to*-infinitive to express the same idea.

It would be well worth the extra expense *in order to be* sure ......

The negative form is with *in order not* + *to*-infinitive.

He drove quickly *in order not to be* late.

Notice that we also use *avoid* + gerund to express this idea.

He drove quickly *to avoid being* late.

Now combine the following pairs of sentences to form one sentence, modelling your answers on the examples given above.

a I put on my glasses. I wanted to read the notice, which was in small print.

b She's going for a walk. She wants to get some fresh air.

c He deliberately crossed the road. He didn't want to speak to me.

d I shall have to go to the library. I want to look the word up in the dictionary.

e He's gone to the bank. He wants to cash a cheque.

f They went to a cheap hotel. They didn't want to spend a lot of money.

g We ought to leave now. We want to be sure of getting a seat.

h I must stop at the tobacconist's. I want to buy some cigarettes.

i John went to the airport. He wanted to see his brother off.

j I'm going to whisper. I don't want to disturb the others.

8

A car drew up outside the Swan Hotel and a young man got out. Pausing only for an instant to see that he had come to the right place, he went into the hotel and rang the bell on the counter of the bar.

5 Mrs Crump, the landlady, who was busy in the kitchen at the time, hurried out, wiping her hands. The young man raised his hat.

"Excuse me," he said. "I'm looking for my uncle, Mr White. I believe he is staying here."

"He *was* staying here," Mrs Crump corrected him. "But I'm 10 afraid that he went back to London yesterday."

"Oh dear," said the young man, looking disappointed. "I understood that he was going to stay here until the end of the month. At least, that is what his servant told me when I rang up his house."

"Quite right," said Mrs Crump. "He intended to stay here the 15 whole of July, as he always does. But yesterday he got a telegram to say that one of his relatives was ill. So he caught the train back to London immediately."

"I wish he had let me know," the young man said. "I wrote him a letter saying that I was coming. I've had all this trouble for 20 nothing. Well, since he isn't here, there is no point in waiting."

He thanked Mrs Crump and went out. Mrs Crump went to the window and watched him drive off. When his car was out of sight, she called out:

"You can come out now, Mr White. He's gone."

25 Mr White came out of the kitchen, where he had been waiting.

"Many thanks, Mrs Crump," he said, laughing. "You did that very well. These nephews of mine never give me any peace. That young man is the worst of them all. As you see, when he needs money, he even follows me into the country. Well, perhaps next 30 time he won't warn me by writing me a letter!"

1 *Choose the best answer.*

  a This story is about a man who
    (i) did not like his nephew
    (ii) did not want to meet his nephew
    (iii) was not able to meet his nephew
    (iv) wanted to spend a quiet holiday in the country
  b When his nephew came to the hotel, the man

(i) avoided giving him any money
(ii) caught the train back to London
(iii) went to see a sick relative
(iv) hid in the kitchen

2 *Answer the following questions briefly, in your own words as far as possible. Use one complete sentence for each answer.*
a How did Mrs Crump know that someone had entered the hotel?
b Why did Mrs Crump watch the young man drive off?

3 *Answer these questions, using only short form answers.*
a Had the young man come to the right hotel?
b Had Mr White been to this hotel for his holiday in other years?

4 *Complete the following sentences. Your answers must be related to the ideas contained in the passage.*

a When Mrs Crump heard the bell ring, ...
b The young man came to the Swan Hotel expecting ......
c The young man was disappointed when he heard that ......
d Mr White did not come out of the kitchen until ......
e Mr White thanked Mrs Crump for ......

5 *Choose the best explanation according to the context.*
a *drew up* (1) means
   (i) waited   (ii) stopped
   (iii) paused   (iv) appeared
b *no point in* (20) means
   (i) no time to   (ii) boring
   (iii) unnecessary   (iv) serves no purpose

6 *Composition* Imagine that you were Mr White. Describe in not more than 100 words the scene which took place between your nephew and Mrs Crump. Do not include any ideas which are not in the passage. Use your own words as far as possible.

7 *Notice this sentence:*
   Mrs Crump ...... *watched* him *drive off*.
In this pattern the verb of perception (*see, hear, notice,* etc.) is followed by an object (noun or pronoun) + the infinitive without *to*. The infinitive indicates that we are interested in the completed action:

22

I *heard* the bell *ring* (i.e. The bell rang. I heard it).
Compare this with the pattern where the present participle is used (see Exercise 6 on pages 82–3); here the interest is in the continuous nature of the action:

I *heard* the bell *ringing*.

The infinitive pattern is also used with a number of other verbs: *make, let, help, know*.

She *made (let, helped)* her husband *cut down* the tree.

Now complete these sentences by choosing a suitable verb from the list given at the foot of the exercise.

a He closed the door quietly so that no one would hear him ......

b Who actually saw the accident ...... ?

c Do you know what made her ...... her mind ?

d Just watch me ...... that wall.

e Let me ...... what I am saying before you interrupt.

f Nobody offered to help Joan ...... the dirty cups.

g Did anyone notice the bird ...... its cage ?

h I've never heard her ...... a kind word.

i He felt the heavy box ...... his hands and ...... the ground.

j Have you ever known him ...... a joke ?

change	go out	say
fall to	happen	slip from
finish	jump over	wash up
fly out of	make	

9

Dear Rosemary,

5   I was delighted to get your letter this morning. I really ought to have written to you—it was my turn, I know—but I have been terribly busy. The children seem to take up all my time. I am thinking of sending Ann to a nursery school. She'll be four next month. Baby has just started to walk and doesn't give me a moment's
10 peace. But you know what it is like! How are all your children? I'm sure they love living in the country.

I'm afraid we can't come over to see you next Sunday, as you suggest. Tom's mother is coming to spend the day with us. What about the Sunday after that—the twenty-second? We are free that
15 day and should love to come. We're longing to see your new house.

Let me know, then, if the Sunday after next suits you. May we come for lunch? We'd like to leave fairly early in the evening to avoid the heavy traffic on the roads.

Love from us all,
Edna.

20

Birch Cottage,
Little Tipping, Kent.
October 15th.

Dear Edna,

25 Yes, we'd love you to come the Sunday after next. And please do come for lunch. I'll try to think of something really special to cook. Ted says you can help him in the garden. He wasn't so pleased when I said that the children would help, too! I'm looking forward to seeing the baby. Can he really walk already? Time certainly flies!

30 We've had a lot of work to do in the house, but it has been worth it. It is good to be living in the country once more. I never enjoyed town life, as you know. You ought to look for a house in the country. But I suppose Tom wouldn't like the long journey to work every day.

35 We shall expect you about midday. Look after yourself and don't work too hard. Love to you both.

Rosemary.

1 *Choose the best answer.*

   a Edna could not go to see Rosemary the following Sunday because
     (i) she was afraid of the traffic
     (ii) Tom's mother was coming to see them that day
     (iii) she preferred to come on the twenty-second
     (iv) she was terribly busy with the children

   b Rosemary said: "Time certainly flies" because
     (i) Edna was coming to see them the Sunday after next
     (ii) she had never seen the baby
     (iii) there was not enough time to do all the work in the house
     (iv) she could hardly believe that the baby could walk already

2 *Answer the following questions briefly, in your own words as far as possible. Use one complete sentence for each answer.*

   a How soon did Edna answer Rosemary's letter?
   b How were Edna and Tom going to travel to the country?

3 *Answer these questions, using only short form answers.*

   a Had Edna already seen Rosemary's new house in the country?
   b Had Rosemary lived in the country before?

4 *Complete the following sentences. Your answers must be related to the ideas contained in the passage.*

   a Edna had not had time to answer Rosemary's letter because ......
   b Edna wrote to say that they could not come the following Sunday because ......
   c Edna suggested instead that ......
   d Ted did not want the children ......
   e At the end of her letter, Rosemary told Edna ......

5 *Choose the best explanation according to the context.*

   a *terribly* (7) means

     (i) extremely   (ii) frighteningly
     (iii) unusually   (iv) unpleasantly

   b *once more* (31) means

     (i) more than once   (ii) for a long time
     (iii) again   (iv) at last

6 *Composition* Imagine you were Edna. Write a letter of about 100 words to a friend describing your Sunday in the country with Rosemary and Ted. In your letter refer to (i) the cottage, (ii) Tom's

garden, (iii) the lunch and (iv) the journey back to Plumpton in the evening.

7 *Notice this sentence:*
   I really *ought to have written* to you.
Ought to or *should* with a perfect infinitive is used to express an obligation which was not carried out. Here is another example:

Helen $\begin{Bmatrix} ought\ to \\ should \end{Bmatrix}$ *have gone* to the dentist's yesterday (but she didn't go).

The negative form expresses disapproval of an action which was actually performed.
   You *oughtn't to (shouldn't) have bought* that hat.

Now complete these sentences.

a This meat isn't done. You should ...... (*cook*) it longer.
b We'll miss the train. We ought to ...... (*leave*) earlier.
c Why did you let her go alone ? Someone should ...... (*go*) with her.
d I'm surprised he did that. He ought to ...... (*know*) better.
e The accident was his fault. He shouldn't ...... (*drive*) so quickly.
f You ought to ...... (*ask*) their permission before you borrowed it.
g We should ...... (*bring*) a map. Now we're lost.
h All my shirts are dirty. They should ...... (*send**) to the laundry yesterday.
i They oughtn't to ...... (*sell*) their house. Now they've nowhere to live.
j It's too late now. I should ...... (*tell**) earlier.

* Use the Passive form.

Shortly after the war, my brother and I were invited to spend a few days' holiday with an uncle who had just returned from abroad. He had rented a cottage in the country, although he rarely spent much time there. We understood the reason for this after our
5 arrival: the cottage had no comfortable furniture in it, many of the windows were broken and the roof leaked, making the whole house damp.

On our first evening, we sat around the fire after supper listening to the stories which our uncle had to tell of his many adventures
10 in distant countries. I was so tired after the long train journey that I would have preferred to go to bed; but I could not bear to miss any of my uncle's exciting tales.

He was just in the middle of describing a rather terrifying experience he had once had when his small sailing boat was carried out
15 to sea in a storm, when there was a loud crash from the bedroom above, the one where my brother and I were going to sleep.

"It sounds as if the roof has fallen in!" exclaimed my uncle, with a loud laugh.

When we got to the top of the stairs and opened the bedroom
20 door, we could see nothing at first because of the thick clouds of dust which filled the room. When the dust began to clear, a strange sight met our eyes. A large part of the ceiling had collapsed, falling right on to the pillow of my bed. I was glad that I had stayed up late to listen to my uncle's stories, otherwise I should certainly
25 have been seriously injured, perhaps killed.

That night we all slept on the floor of the sitting-room downstairs, not wishing to risk our lives by sleeping under a roof which might at any moment collapse on our heads. We left for London the very next morning and my uncle gave up his cottage in the country. This
30 was not the kind of adventure he cared for either!

1 *Choose the best answer.*
  a The writer did not go to bed immediately after supper because
     (i) it was pleasant sitting round the fire
     (ii) his uncle terrified him with his stories
     (iii) he wanted to hear all his uncle's exciting stories
     (iv) his uncle made him listen to his stories

b It was quite clear that the ceiling had fallen in
  (i) when they opened the bedroom door
  (ii) after the dust had begun to clear
  (iii) as soon as they heard the crash
  (iv) when they reached the top of the stairs

2 *Answer the following questions briefly, using your own words as far as possible. Use one complete sentence for each answer.*
  a Why didn't the writer's uncle spend much time in his cottage?
  b Why were they afraid to sleep upstairs that night?

3 *Answer these questions, using only short form answers.*
  a Was the writer's uncle amused when he heard the loud crash?
  b Did the writer's uncle continue living in his cottage?

4 *Complete the following sentences. Your answers must be related to the ideas contained in the passage.*

  a The writer's uncle did not spend much time in the cottage which ......
  b The cottage was damp because ......
  c Although the writer was tired, ...
  d ...... right on to the pillow of the bed where ......
  e If the writer had gone to bed early, ...

5 *Choose the best explanation according to the context.*
  a leaked (6) means
(i) was beginning to fall down	(ii) let the rain in
(iii) needed to be repaired	(iv) was in bad condition
  b injured (25) means
(i) badly hurt	(ii) damaged
(iii) struck	(iv) wounded

6 *Composition* Imagine that you were the writer's uncle. Write a short account, in about 120 words, of the experience you had when your sailing boat was carried out to sea in a storm.

7 *Notice this sentence:*

> I was glad that I had stayed up late to listen to my uncle's stories, *otherwise* I should certainly have been seriously injured.

Here *otherwise* is equivalent to: If I hadn't stayed up late, I . . .
The use of the conjunction enables us to avoid repetition. Here are some more examples:

> Be quiet, *otherwise* (i.e. if you are not quiet) I won't tell you a story.

> You'll have to work harder, *otherwise* (i.e. if you don't work harder) you won't pass the examination.

Now combine the following pairs of sentences by means of *otherwise*, following the models given above.

a Be more careful. If you aren't more careful, you'll burn your fingers.

b I caught hold of her hand. If I hadn't caught hold of her hand, she would have slipped and fallen.

c They must have gone out. If they weren't out, they would open the door.

d Tom wants a higher salary. If he doesn't get a higher salary, he is going to resign.

e Take an umbrella with you. If you don't take an umbrella, you may get wet.

f We must save more money. If we don't save more money, we shan't be able to go away on holiday.

g They had a map. If they hadn't had a map, they would have lost their way.

h Look out! If you don't look out, you'll get run over.

i The children must have been tired. If they hadn't been tired, they wouldn't have gone to sleep at once.

j You'll have to take more exercise. If you don't take more exercise, you'll get fat.

11

Mrs Brown was tired after her day's shopping in London, so she went into a restaurant for a cup of tea before catching the train home. When she had ordered her tea, she suddenly remembered that she had to buy some medicine for her husband, who had a
5 cough.

"Is there a chemist's near here?" she asked the waiter.

"Yes, madam," the waiter said, "it's only about three minutes' walk away. Turn right when you go out of the restaurant, then take the second turning to the left. You'll find a big chemist's about
10 a hundred yards up the road on the right-hand side. It closes at five, but if you hurry, you'll just get there in time."

Mrs Brown followed the waiter's directions carefully and found the chemist's shop without any difficulty. She bought the cough mixture and started to make her way back to the restaurant. But
15 after she had walked for about ten minutes and there was still no sign of the restaurant, she realised that she must have made a mistake.

"Oh! I am stupid!" said Mrs Brown. "I've left all my shopping in the restaurant and now I'm lost."

20 She was still wondering what to do when a policeman came up and asked if he could help. Mrs Brown explained what had happened.

"Well, first of all," said the policeman, "we had better go back as far as the chemist's."

25 "Now," suggested the policeman, when they got to the chemist's, "let's go in this direction. It leads to the main road, where we shall probably find your restaurant."

When they reached the main road, the policeman said:

"I think you'll find the restaurant you are looking for along there,
30 on the opposite side of the road."

Mrs Brown thanked the policeman for his help.

"I can't understand how I went wrong," she said.

The policeman smiled.

"It's quite easy," he said, "to get lost in a big city like London."

1 *Choose the best answer.*
   a Mrs Brown called herself stupid because
      (i) she had walked for ten minutes before she realised that she had lost her way
      (ii) she had managed to lose her way just coming back from the chemist's shop
      (iii) she had left her shopping in a restaurant which she could not find
      (iv) she had taken the wrong road back to the chemist's

2 *Answer the following questions briefly, in your own words as far as possible. Use one complete sentence for each answer.*
   a Why had Mrs Brown come to London?
   b How far was the chemist's from the restaurant?
   c When did Mrs Brown realise that she had made a mistake?

3 *Answer these questions, using only short form answers.*
   a Did the waiter give Mrs Brown good directions?
   b Did Mrs Brown reach the chemist's in time?
   c Did the policeman come with Mrs Brown as far as the chemist's?

4 *Complete the following sentences. Your answers must be related to the ideas contained in the passage.*
   a Mrs Brown went to the restaurant for a cup of tea because ......
   b Mrs Brown's husband had a bad cough, so ......
   c Mrs Brown had to hurry to the chemist's because ......
   d The policeman came up to Mrs Brown and asked her: "...... ?"
   e Mrs Brown might not have found the restaurant again if ......

5 *Choose the best explanation according to the context.*
   a *in time* (11) means
      (i) eventually   (ii) before it closes
      (iii) punctually   (iv) at the right time

6 *Find words or phrases in the passage which mean much the same as the following.*
   a instructions how to get to a place
   b to return
   c made a mistake

7 *Composition* Imagine that you were the policeman mentioned in the passage. Describe in not more than 90 words what happened

from the time you first saw Mrs Brown until you took her to the main road. Do not include any ideas which are not in the passage. Use your own words as far as possible.

8 Complete the following sentences by putting the speaker's words, given in brackets, into Indirect Speech. Follow this model:

Mrs Brown said ...... ("I've left all my shopping in the restaurant.")
Mrs Brown said that she had left all her shopping in the restaurant.

 a Mrs Brown asked the waiter ...... ("Is there a chemist's near here?")
 b The waiter told her ...... ("It's only about three minutes' walk away.")
 c He told her ...... ("Turn right when you go out of the restaurant.")
 d He said ...... ("You'll find a big chemist's about a hundred yards up the road.")
 e He said that the chemist's closed at five, but ...... ("If you hurry, you'll just get there in time.")
 f The policeman said that first of all ...... ("We'd better go back as far as the chemist's.")
 g The policeman took Mrs Brown in the direction of the main road, where he said ...... ("We shall probably find your restaurant.")
 h When they reached the main road, the policeman told Mrs Brown ...... ("I think you'll find the restaurant you are looking for on the opposite side of the road.")
 i Mrs Brown thanked the policeman and said ...... ("I can't understand how I went wrong.")
 j The policeman smiled and said ...... ("It's quite easy to get lost in a big city like London.")

As the train approached the seaside town where I was going to spend my holidays, I went into the corridor to stretch my legs. I stayed there a short while, breathing in the fresh sea air and exchanging a few words with one of the passengers, whom I had
5 met earlier on the station platform.

When I turned to go back to my seat, I happened to glance into the compartment next to mine. Sitting there was a man who many years before had been my neighbour. He was a great talker, I remembered; it used to take hours to get away from him once
10 he began a conversation. I was not at all sorry when he went to live in another part of London. We had not met since then, nor did I wish to meet him now, when my holiday was about to begin.

Luckily at that moment he was much too busy talking to the man opposite him to catch sight of me. I slipped back into my compart-
15 ment, took down my two suitcases and carried them to the far end of the corridor so as to be ready to get off the train as soon as it stopped. The moment the train came to a halt, I called a porter, who in no time at all had carried my luggage out of the station and found me a taxi. As I drove towards my small hotel on the outskirts
20 of the town, I breathed a deep sigh of relief at my narrow escape. There was little chance that I should run into my boring ex-neighbour again.

When I reached the hotel, I went straight to my room and rested there until it was time for dinner. Then I went down to the lounge
25 and ordered a drink. I had barely raised the glass to my lips when an all too familiar voice greeted me. I had not escaped from my tiresome neighbour after all! He grasped me warmly by the hand and insisted that we should share a table in the dining-room. "This is a pleasant surprise," he said. "I never expected to see you again
30 after all these years."

1 *Choose the best answer.*
  a This is a story about a man who
    (i) got off the train to avoid meeting an ex-neighbour
    (ii) went with an ex-neighbour to spend a holiday at the seaside
    (iii) tried to get away from an ex-neighbour but did not succeed
    (iv) was surprised to meet his ex-neighbour in a small seaside hotel

2 *Answer the following questions briefly, in your own words as far as possible. Use one complete sentence for each answer.*
   a Why did the writer want to avoid his ex-neighbour?
   b Why did the writer feel sure that he had escaped from his ex-neighbour?
   c What was the writer doing when his ex-neighbour greeted him?

3 *Answer these questions, using only short form answers.*
   a Did the writer speak to anyone in the corridor?
   b Did it take the writer long to get out of the station?
   c Did the writer recognise his ex-neighbour's voice at once?

4 *Complete the following sentences. Your answers must be related to the ideas contained in the passage.*

   a The writer had not seen his ex-neighbour since ......
   b The writer got back to his compartment without being seen because ......
   c The porter not only ...... but also ......
   d The hotel where ...... was on the outskirts of the town.
   e "We must ......," said the ex-neighbour, grasping ......

5 *Choose the best explanation according to the context.*
   a *tiresome* (27) means
       (i) weary   (ii) talkative
       (iii) boring   (iv) sleepy

6 *Find words or phrases in the passage which mean much the same as the following.*
   a returned without being noticed
   b extremely quickly
   c known very well

7 *Composition* Describe in not more than 90 words what the writer of the passage did from the time he went back to his compartment until his ex-neighbour greeted him in the hotel. Do not include any ideas which are not in the passage. Use your own words as far as possible.

8 *Notice this sentence:*
   He found me a taxi.
   This pattern, with the Indirect Object preceding the Direct Object

34

of the verb, is mostly to be found where the Indirect Object is shorter, and consequently less emphatic, than the Direct Object. Compare these two sentences:

I lent him my book.

I lent my book to a student who sits in the front row.

Now complete the following sentences by arranging the two objects given in brackets according to length and degree of emphasis required. For example:

I paid ...... (*the man*) (*the money*).

I paid the man the money.

She wrote ...... (*the headmaster of her son's school*) (*a letter*).

She wrote a letter to the headmaster of her son's school.

a I've just been out to buy ...... (*a friend of mine who is getting married*) (*a wedding present*).

b She made ...... (*me*) (*a nice cup of tea*).

c He gave ...... (*the beggar*) (*all the money he had in his pocket*).

d They are going to give ...... (*the best students in the examination*) (*certificates*).

e Nobody has sent ...... (*me*) (*any Christmas cards*) yet.

f I had to show ...... (*the porter at the entrance to the building*) (*my pass*) before I was allowed in.

g I sent ...... (*the editor of the Literary Monthly*) (*my article*).

h He showed ...... (*us all*) (*a photograph of his eldest daughter*).

i John has never bought ...... (*his wife*) (*a bunch of flowers*).

j She always makes ...... (*anyone who comes to see her*) (*tea*).

13

"You do buy old books, don't you?" asked Fred, putting his parcel down on the shop counter.

"I'll have to see what you've got before I can answer that question," the bookseller said. "Business isn't so good as it used to be.
5 People seem to prefer to buy new books nowadays."

Fred opened his parcel and laid the books out on the counter.

"I don't pretend to know much about books," he said. "I've had these for years, and I haven't even read them. My grandfather left them to me, as a matter of fact. But my wife never stops com-
10 plaining about them. She says they make the house look dirty. So I thought I'd bring them in to show you, just in case there is anything of interest."

In the meantime, the bookseller was picking up the books one by one and examining them. He shook his head.

15 "They're not much good," he said. "I can give you a few pounds for the lot if you want to get rid of them. I can't offer you more, I'm afraid."

When he saw the last book, however, his eyes lit up with excitement.

20 "What is it?" asked Fred.

"Now this *is* worth something," exclaimed the bookseller, turning over the pages. "It's a very rare edition."

He handed the book to Fred, who looked at the title. It was a novel of the last century by an author whose name he had never
25 heard of. Of all the books which he had gathered together to bring to the bookshop, this one had looked the least interesting.

"How much is it worth?" he asked the bookseller.

"How much?" the man repeated. "I can't tell you exactly. But not less than a hundred pounds, I should say. I'm only guessing. It
30 may be worth a lot more."

It was Fred's turn to be excited. He thought of all the wonderful things he could buy with a hundred pounds.

1 *Choose the best answer.*
   a Fred took the old books to the bookseller because
      (i) he never had time to read them
      (ii) his wife did not like having them in the house
      (iii) he wanted to find out what they were worth

(iv) he expected to get some money for them

2 *Answer the following questions briefly, in your own words as far as possible. Use one complete sentence for each answer.*
a How much did the bookseller first offer Fred for the books?
b Why was the last book worth a lot of money?
c How much did the bookseller think that the last book might be worth?

3 *Answer these questions, using only short form answers.*
a Did the bookseller find it easy to sell old books?
b Did the bookseller examine all the books?
c Did Fred expect the last book to be worth a lot of money?

4 *Complete the following sentences. Your answers must be related to the ideas contained in the passage.*

a As he put his parcel down on the counter, Fred asked the bookseller whether ......
b Fred laid the books out on the counter so that ......
c Fred hadn't read the books, although ......
d Fred ...... but the bookseller couldn't tell him exactly.
e Fred was excited at the thought of ......

5 *Choose the best explanation according to the context.*
a *for the lot* (16) means
  (i) for many of them   (ii) for most of them
  (iii) for all of them   (iv) for some of them

6 *Find words or phrases in the passage which mean much the same as the following.*
a at the present time   b grumbling
c became bright

7 *Composition* Imagine that you were Fred. Describe in not more than 90 words what happened from the time the bookseller first began to examine the books until he told you how much the last book might be worth. Do not include any ideas which are not in the passage. Use your own words as far as possible.

8 *Notice this sentence:*
Business isn't so good as it *used to be*.

37

Here *used* describes a state of affairs which lasted for some time in the past, but has since changed. *Used* is also employed to indicate habits which have been given up.

Here are some more examples of its use:

I don't smoke so much as I *used to*.

He *used to go* to work by train. Now he goes by car.

Mary *usedn't* (or *never used*) to have such long hair.

Now complete the following sentences by using *used* with the *to*-infinitive of a suitable verb chosen from the list given at the foot of the exercise.

a Our neighbour Jackson had a dog which ...... all night.

b The bell ...... at the end of every lesson.

c As soon as he was given any money, he ...... it.

d That's the cottage where Wordsworth ......

e When we were children, it ...... us an hour to walk home from school.

f On summer evenings we ...... in the garden after dinner.

g He eats too much . He ...... * so fat.

h I ...... reading the letters you wrote me while you were abroad.

i Eggs are expensive now, but I can remember when they ...... twopence each.

j The books Fred sold ...... his grandfather.

bark	enjoy	sit
be	live	spend
belong to	ring	take
cost		

* Use the negative form.

38

14

The clock struck a quarter past nine as Mary hurried into the big block of offices where she was going to work. Her bus had crawled through the dense city traffic, making her a few minutes late for her very first job. She resolved to leave home earlier the next day.

5 Inside the building she had to wait once again, this time for the lift to take her up to the sixth floor. When at last she reached the door marked "*J. King, Manager*", she knocked rather nervously and waited. There was no answer. She tapped on the door again, but still there was no reply. From inside the next office she could hear
10 the sound of voices, so she opened the door and went in.

Although it was without doubt the same office she had been shown into when she had come for an interview with Mr King two weeks before, on that morning it looked quite different. In fact it hardly looked like an office at all. All the employees were standing
15 about, chatting and smoking. At the far end of the room a man must have just told a very funny story, for there was a loud burst of laughter just as Mary came in. For a moment she thought that they were laughing at her.

Then one of the men looked at his watch, clapped his hands
20 and said something to the others. Immediately they all went to their desks and, in the space of a few seconds, everyone was working busily. No one took any notice of Mary at all. At last she went up to the man who was sitting at the desk nearest the door and explained that this was her first day in the office. Hardly looking up from his
25 work, he told her to take a seat near him and wait for Mr King, who would arrive at any moment. Then Mary realised that the day's work in the office began just before Mr King arrived. Later she found out that he came up every morning from the country on the same train, arriving promptly in the office at 9.35, so that his staff knew precisely
30 when to start work.

1 *Choose the best answer.*
   a Mary hardly recognised the office she went into because
      (i) she had been there only once before
      (ii) nobody was doing any work
      (iii) she was still feeling very nervous
      (iv) people were making so much noise in the office

2 *Answer the following questions briefly, in your own words as far as possible. Use one complete sentence for each answer.*
  a How did Mary know that she was late?
  b How did Mary get to the sixth floor?
  c Whose voices could Mary hear from the next office?

3 *Answer these questions, using only short form answers.*
  a Was Mr King in his office when Mary knocked on the door?
  b Were the people in the office laughing at Mary?
  c Did Mr King live in the city?

4 *Complete the following sentences. Your answers must be related to the ideas contained in the passage.*
  a Mary resolved to leave home earlier the next day in order to ......
  b The office Mary was going to work in was on the sixth floor, so ......
  c It hardly looked like an office that morning because ......
  d One of the men clapped his hands and said: "......"
  e Mary had to wait for Mr King because ......

5 *Choose the best explanation according to the context.*
  a resolved (4) means
     (i) found a solution   (ii) thought about
     (iii) agreed   (iv) was determined

6 *Find words or phrases in the passage which mean much the same as the following.*
  a went very slowly   b paid any attention to
  c exactly

7 *Composition* Imagine that you were Mary. Describe in not more

  than 90 words what you did and saw from the time you entered the office until the man told you to sit down. Do not include any ideas which are not in the passage. Use your own words as far as possible.

8 *Notice this sentence:*
  A man *must have* just *told* a very funny story, for there was a loud burst of laughter.
  Must + a perfect infinitive is used to indicate a very probable con-

clusion drawn from a certain situation. In this case, it is probable, almost certain, that the man had told a very funny story because everyone laughed.

Now complete these sentences by using *must* + the perfect infinitive of the verb given in brackets.

a The streets are wet. It ...... (*rain*) in the night.
b I didn't hear anything. I ...... (*be*) asleep.
c Mary got the job. She ...... (*make*) a good impression.
d John promised to telephone. I wonder why he hasn't. He ...... (*forget*).
e Someone ...... (*leave*) the cage door open. The bird has got out.
f That's a lovely dress you're wearing. It ...... (*cost*) a lot of money.
g Mr King is late this morning. He ...... (*miss*) the train.
h You look pleased. You ...... (*have*) some good news.
i I know how this book ends. I ...... (*read*) it before.
j You ...... (*make*) a mistake. Mr Brown doesn't live in this house.

15

It was dark in the attic, as Miss Manning had warned him. Weston found the small window in the roof and forced it open, thus letting in more light. He could just make out the boxes which Miss Manning had told him about.

5   "When my father died," Miss Manning had said, "his large library was sold up. His papers, and some other possessions of no great value, were stored in boxes and put up in the attic. They've been there ever since. I don't suppose the room has been opened for over ten years."

10   "What about his diaries?" asked Weston. "In one of his letters to a friend, Colonel Manning mentions that he kept a diary."

"I don't remember seeing any diaries," said Miss Manning, with a puzzled look on her face. "Of course, he may have destroyed them before his last illness. Otherwise they must be in those boxes in 15 the attic."

"I see," murmured Weston. "In that case, will you allow me to examine those boxes? If I can find the diaries, I'll be able to write a much more complete account of your father's life."

"Certainly you may," said Miss Manning. "You can't imagine 20 how thrilled I am that anyone should want to write a book about father. I would have taken more care of his papers if I had known."

After searching through a number of drawers, Miss Manning found the key to the attic.

"You won't find it easy to see up there," she said as she handed 25 him the key. "There's a small window in the roof, but I expect that it will be too dirty to see through."

There were about a dozen boxes in all. Weston did not know where to begin. He opened first one, then the other, but found nothing that looked like diaries. Then he decided to try the largest 30 box. It was full of papers. As he turned these over, a bundle of exercise books, tied together with string, caught his eye. On the cover of the top one were written the words "DIARY, 1935-36".

1 *Choose the best answer.*
  a Weston wanted to find Colonel Manning's diaries because
    (i) he was interested in the colonel's private life
    (ii) they were mentioned in one of the colonel's letters
    (iii) he thought that the colonel's daughter was not taking enough

care of her father's papers

(iv) he wanted to write as complete as possible an account of the colonel's life

2 *Answer the following questions briefly, in your own words as far as possible. Use one complete sentence for each answer.*
   a Why was it dark in the attic?
   b When were the boxes put up in the attic?
   c Who was Weston?

3 *Answer these questions, using only short form answers.*
   a Were Colonel Manning's books also put up in the attic?
   b Did Miss Manning give Weston permission to look in the boxes?
   c Did Miss Manning find the key to the attic quickly?

4 *Complete the following sentences. Your answers must be related to the ideas contained in the passage.*
   a There was more light in the attic after ......
   b Miss Manning looked puzzled when Weston ......
   c Miss Manning tho ;ht that ...... before his last illness.
   d Weston wanted to find the diaries in order to ......
   e When Weston opened the largest box, he found that ......

5 *Choose the best explanation according to the context.*
   a murmured (16) means
      (i) grumbled   (ii) said in a low voice
      (iii) muttered   (iv) admitted

6 *Find words or phrases in the passage which means much the same as the following.*
   a see the difficulty   *b* not worth very much
   c attracted his attention

7 *Composition* Imagine that you were Miss Manning. Write a letter of about 100 words to your sister, telling her about Weston's visit and how he discovered the diaries. Include appropriate details from the passage. Use your own words as far as possible.

8 *Notice this sentence:*
   He *may have destroyed* them before his last illness.
   May + a perfect infinitive is used to indicate a possibility, usually

43

in the past, about which we are uncertain. In this case, Miss Manning is not sure whether her father destroyed the diaries or not.

Now complete the following sentences by using *may* + the perfect infinitive of the verb given in brackets.

a I ...... (*tell*) you this story before. Stop me if I have.

b If the book isn't on the shelf, someone ...... (*borrow*) it.

c The man who lives in that house is an artist by the name of Long. You ...... (*hear*) of him.

d Let's go out in about half an hour's time. The rain ...... (*stop*) by then.

e I can't remember what happened to the picture. It ...... (*give away* ★).

f She seemed to be speaking the truth but, for all I know, she ...... (*tell*) me a lie.

g After that we don't know what Brown did. He ...... (*stay*) at home, as he says, or he ...... (*go out*).

h Then I heard something moving under the bed. Of course it...... (*be*) only a mouse.

i If he isn't on this train, he ...... (*decide*) not to come after all.

j The man ...... (*call*★) Robinson. I really don't remember.

★ Use the Passive form.

16

Dear Mr Fenton,

5 On May 1st we are planning to hold a dinner to celebrate the
fifth anniversary of the Selmore Literary Society and I have been
asked by our committee to invite you to be the guest of honour
on this occasion. Since you came to live in our town last year,
you have always shown a great deal of interest in our activities
10 and you are without doubt our most popular speaker. We shall
all be delighted as well as highly honoured if you can once again
find the time to spend an evening in our company. I will send you
further details as soon as I hear from you. I hope you will be able
to accept this invitation.

15   Yours sincerely,
                                 J. N. Edwards.
                                 Honorary Secretary,
                                 Selmore Literary Society.

                                 Scott Villa,
20   Selmore
                                 April 12th, 1963

Dear Mr Edwards,

Thank you for your letter of April 7th, which I am answering
on behalf of my husband. Apparently you have not heard that about
25 a month ago my husband was taken seriously ill, as a result of overwork. Although he is now much better, the doctor has ordered him
to take a complete rest for at least three months. As a matter of
fact we are leaving for the Continent as soon as he is fit to travel
and it is unlikely that we shall return to England before the end of
30 July.

In view of this, I regret that my husband is unable to accept
this kind invitation to the dinner which your society is holding on
May 1st. He has asked me, however, to send his very best wishes for
the success of the occasion and says that he hopes to be with you
35 again in the autumn.
                                 Yours sincerely,
                                 Lydia Fenton.

1 *Choose the best answer.*

   a Mrs Fenton refused the invitation on behalf of her husband because

    (i) he was seriously ill

    (ii) he was recovering from a serious illness

    (iii) he was going to have a holiday abroad

    (iv) the doctor had ordered him to stay in bed for three months

2 *Answer the following questions briefly, in your own words as far as possible. Use one complete sentence for each answer.*

  a When was the Selmore Literary Society founded?

  b Why was Mr Fenton asked to be the guest of honour?

  c How long had Mr Fenton been ill?

3 *Answer these questions, using only short form answers.*

  a Had Mr Fenton lived in Selmore for a long time?

  b Had Mr Fenton attended previous meetings of the Selmore Literary Society?

  c Were the Fentons intending to stay in England that summer?

4 *Complete the following sentences. Your answer must be related to the ideas contained in the passage.*

  a The Selmore Literary Society was planning to have a dinner on May 1st because ......

  b Mr Edwards promised to send further details of the dinner as soon as ......

  c Mrs Fenton answered Mr Edward's letter on behalf of her husband because ......

  d "Your husband ......," the doctor told Mrs Fenton.

  e If Mr Fenton had not been taken ill, he ......

5 *Choose the best explanation according to the context.*

  a fit (28) means

    (i) suitable   (ii) ready

    (iii) good enough   (iv) well enough

6 *Find words or phrases in the passage which mean much the same as the following.*

  a liked by everyone   *b* greatly

  c it seems (that)

7 *Composition* Imagine that you were Mr Edwards. Write a letter of about 75 words conveying to Mrs Fenton your sympathy on learning of her husband's illness.

8 *Notice these sentences:*

I *hope* you will be able to accept this invitation.

I *regret* that my husband is unable to accept. . . .

There are a number of verbs in English, such as *see, hear, like, know, understand, remember, believe,* etc., which are rarely found in the continuous forms. These verbs denote a variety of actions or states which for the most part are involuntary.

Here are some more examples:

I *like* Mary's new dress.

John *doesn't understand* what you are saying.

They *want* to stay at home.

Other common verbs used in this way are: *seem, look* (= *seem*), *belong to, contain, matter, mean.*

Now complete the following sentences by using the correct form of the verb, Simple Present or Present Continuous.

a I ...... (*know*) I have seen this film, but I ...... (*not, remember*) what it is about.

b I ...... (*think*) she ...... (*wash*) her hair.

c ...... you ...... (*know*) what this word ...... (*mean*)?

d I ...... (*see*) you are busy. What ...... you ...... (*do*)?

e That policeman ...... (*look*) as if he ...... (*want*) us to stop.

f I ...... (*think*) someone ...... (*knock*) on the door.

g That coat she ...... (*wear*) today ...... (*belong to*) her sister.

h I ...... (*hope*) those children ...... (*know*) how to swim.

i ...... anyone ...... (*know*) what this envelope ...... (*contain*)?

j It ...... (*not, matter*) if they ...... (*not, like*) it.

17

A small crowd had gathered round the entrance to the park. His curiosity aroused, Robert crossed the road to see what was happening. He found that the centre of attraction was an old man with a performing monkey. The monkey's tricks, he soon discovered, were
5 in no way remarkable so, after throwing a few pennies in the dirty hat which the man had placed on the pavement, Robert began to move off, along with other members of the crowd.

At this point the man suddenly let out a loud cry. Everyone turned to see what had happened. The man was bending over his
10 monkey, which now lay quite still on the pavement. He picked up the apparently lifeless body and, holding it close to him, began to weep. A young man stepped forward from the crowd and, taking some money from his pocket, dropped it into the hat. Robert and several other people did likewise, until the pennies in the hat
15 were covered with silver coins. Meanwhile, the man continued to hold the dead monkey in his arms and seemed to take no notice of what was going on about him.

A few months later, Robert came across the old man again in another part of the city. The man had a monkey, bought no doubt
20 with the money which the crowd had given him. It did not, however, seem any better at its tricks than the previous one. Robert was pleased to see that the old man was still able to earn a living, though on this occasion, having partly paid for the monkey out of his own pocket, he did not feel inclined to throw any money into the hat.

25 But the performance was not yet over! Once again the old man let out a loud cry. Once again the monkey lay still on the pavement. The man picked up the "dead" monkey and clutching it in his arms began to weep. The same young man stepped forward and threw some money into the hat. Again the crowd followed suit—except
30 for Robert. Smiling to himself, he went on his way, amazed at the man's audacity.

1 *Choose the best answer.*

  a Robert did not throw any money into the hat the second time because

   (i) there was enough money in it already
   (ii) he had seen the monkey's tricks before
   (iii) the monkey's tricks were not very good

(iv) he knew that the monkey was not really dead

2 *Answer the following questions briefly, in your own words as far as possible. Use one complete sentence for each answer.*
   a What was the crowd round the entrance to the park doing?
   b Why did the crowd soon begin to move off?
   c What was the old man doing while the crowd threw money into his hat?

3 *Answer these questions, using only short form answers.*
   a Did the people throw a lot of money into the hat when they thought that the monkey was dead?
   b Was there much money in the hat already?
   c Did the old man thank the crowd for throwing money into his hat?

4 *Complete the following sentences. Your answers must be related to the ideas contained in the passage.*
   a ...... for people to throw money into.
   b The old man let out a loud cry in order to ......
   c It was a young man who first ...... and ...... Then Robert and the others did likewise.
   d Robert thought that ...... with the money which the crowd had given him.
   e Robert didn't think that the tricks of the new monkey ......

5 *Choose the best explanation according to the context.*
   a *likewise* (14) means
      (i) the sensible thing   (ii) the same thing
      (iii) willingly   (iv) more or less the same

6 *Find words or phrases in the passage which mean much the same as the following.*
   a excited   *b* without moving
   c holding very tight

7 *Composition* Imagine that you were Robert. Write a letter of about 100 words to a friend, explaining the trick which the old man played on the crowd. Use your own words as far as possible.

8 *Notice this sentence:*
The man *continued to hold* the dead monkey in his arms.

49

In this pattern the verb is followed by the *to*-infinitive.
Here are two more examples:

Does she *want to go* to bed early?

They were *trying* hard *not to laugh*.

Compare this with the pattern where the verb is followed by a gerund (see Exercise 7 on page 10):

The children *enjoy playing* in the park.

Now complete the following sentences by choosing a suitable verb from the list given at the foot of the exercise.

a Don't forget ...... the light before you go to bed.

b The door was locked, so he tried ...... the house through the window.

c The man refused ...... the policeman his name and address.

d You promised ...... me a newspaper when you went out shopping.

e Mary wants ...... either a nurse or a secretary when she leaves school.

f When I spoke to him in English, he pretended ...... what I was saying.

g Tom hopes ...... writing his letters by four o'clock.

h Even when I have a lot of work to do, you never offer ...... me.

i In the end they decided ...... by sea.

j I meant ...... you to the party, but I forgot.

become	help	tell
buy	invite	travel*
finish	switch off	understand*
get into		

★ Use the negative form.

50

18

"Now, sir," said Inspector Robinson, drawing a chair up close to the injured man's bed and sitting down, "I hope you feel well enough to answer a few questions."

"Yes, of course," said Topham. He sat up in bed. The nurse
5 placed another pillow behind his head and left the room.

"First of all," said the inspector, opening his notebook, "we have to establish your identity."

Topham looked astonished. "My identity? Don't you even know who I am? How long have I been lying in hospital?"

10 "Three days," the inspector told him. "But we found no papers on you at all. Whoever attacked you also stole your wallet."

"But what about my car?" asked Topham. "Surely you could have found out my identity from that?"

"Your car was stolen, too," the inspector explained patiently.
15 "So, you see, we've been completely in the dark. You were discovered on Tuesday night lying unconscious in the car park of the Sun Inn, where you had stopped for dinner that evening. That is all we know about you. Anyway, perhaps now you can give us the information we require."

20 Topham told the inspector his name and address.

"You're not married, are you, sir?" the inspector asked.

"I'm a widower," Topham said. "I've lived alone ever since my wife died three years ago. This year, as always, I went to spend my holidays by the sea. I decided to come back early because of the
25 bad weather. On my way back to London I stopped at the Sun Inn for dinner. . . ."

The inspector nodded and waited for Topham to go on.

"It was raining pretty hard when I came out of the hotel. I dashed towards the car park, where I had left my car. I had just
30 unlocked the door and was getting in when a man stepped out of the shadows and asked me for a lift to London. Before I had time to reply, he attacked me. After that I can remember nothing until I woke up in hospital."

1 *Choose the best answer.*
  a The inspector did not know who Topham was because
    (i) they had not caught the man who attacked him
    (ii) his car had been stolen

     (iii) both his wallet and his car had been stolen
     (iv) he had been unconscious

2 *Answer the following questions briefly, in your own words as far as possible. Use one complete sentence for each answer.*
  a Why did Topham look astonished?
  b Where was Topham attacked?
  c What was Topham doing when he was attacked?

3 *Answer these questions, using only short form answers.*
  a Was Topham willing to answer the inspector's questions?
  b Was the nurse present while the inspector questioned Topham?
  c Was Topham's wife still alive?

4 *Complete the following sentences. Your answers must be related to the ideas contained in the passage.*
  a Inspector Robinson sat down on the chair which he ......
  b Topham was sitting up in bed, so the nurse ......
  c If Topham's car had not been stolen, the police ......
  d Topham dashed towards the car park because ......
  e "......?" asked the man, as he stepped out of the shadows.

5 *Choose the best explanation according to the context.*
  a in the dark (15) means
    (i) at night   (ii) obscure
    (iii) hidden   (iv) not knowing anything

6 *Find words or phrases in the passage which mean much the same as the following.*
  a bringing near to   *b* make certain who a person is
  c hurried

7 *Composition* Imagine that you were Inspector Robinson. Write a short report of about 90 words of what Topham told you. Give Topham's full name and address in your report but otherwise do not include anything which is not in the passage. Use your own words as far as possible.

8 *Notice these sentences:*
    I've lived alone ever *since* my wife died.
    For the last ten days I've been on holiday.

Since is used to indicate the *point* of time at which the action or event began.

I have known him *since* $\begin{cases} \text{last week.} \\ \text{April.} \\ \text{I came to live in this town.} \end{cases}$

For is used to indicate the *period* of time over which an action or event has lasted.

She has been waiting *for* $\begin{cases} \text{ten minutes.} \\ \text{about half an hour.} \\ \text{more than a week.} \end{cases}$

Now write each of the following sentences twice, using either *for* or *since* with the expressions of time given in brackets.

a The inspector has been in Topham's room ...... (*about an hour*) (*the nurse came out*).

b That man has been standing at the corner ...... (*two o'clock*) (*ages*).

c They've been married ...... (*last Easter*) (*just eight years*).

d It hasn't stopped raining ...... (*over twelve hours*) (*last night*).

e We've been at sea now ...... (*three weeks*) (*August 15th*).

f I've been reading *War and Peace* ...... (*Christmas*) (*the last two months*).

g Mr Brown hasn't spoken to his next door neighbour ...... (*twenty years*) (*1945*).

h John has been working in this office ...... (*he left school*) (*nearly eighteen months*).

i No one has lived in this house ...... (*1865*) (*about a century*).

j The postman hasn't brought a letter ...... (*last week*) (*the last week*).

19

We first became aware that something unusual was happening when one of the ship's officers came up to the Chief Engineer, who sat at our table, and spoke to him in a low voice. The Chief Engineer at once stood up and with a brief excuse, which told us nothing, left
5 the dining-room. At first we thought that there had been an accident or that a fire had broken out on board ship, but soon the word went round that a man had been seen floating in the sea. Then we noticed that the ship had slowed down and was beginning to turn round, with rather a violent motion. Some of the passengers did not wait
10 to finish their meal, but at once rushed up on deck. Others crowded round the portholes, making it impossible for us to eat in comfort. There was such confusion in the dining-room that we decided to join those who had gone up on deck.

There we learnt that one of the crew had seen a man in the sea
15 some distance from the ship. He had informed the captain, who at once ordered the ship to be turned round. We were now only two hundred yards or so from the man, and a lifeboat had already been lowered into the sea. In it there were four sailors, who were sitting ready at the oars, an officer and the ship's doctor. The officer shouted
20 an order and the sailors began to row away from the ship. By looking in the same direction as the boat was going, we were able to make out the position of the man in the water. He was clinging to a large piece of wood.

At last, after what seemed to us an age, the lifeboat reached the
25 man and two of the sailors pulled him on board. This was not at all easy, for the sea was rather rough. Then the sailors began to row back to the ship again. The lifeboat was raised out of the water and the rescued man, wrapped in a blanket, was helped out on to the deck. Leaning on the arm of the ship's doctor, but still able to
30 walk in spite of his terrible experience, he was led off to the ship's hospital. As he passed along the deck, everyone cheered loudly.

1 *Choose the best answer.*
   a The people at the writer's table decided to leave the dining-room because
      (i) the ship was turning round rather violently
      (ii) the Chief Engineer had already left

(iii) a man had been seen floating in the sea

(iv) they could not continue their meal in peace

2 *Answer the following questions briefly, in your own words as far as possible. Use one complete sentence for each answer.*

 a Why did some of the passengers crowd round the portholes?

 b How were the people on deck able to make out where the man in the water was?

 c How did the man in the water manage to keep afloat?

3 *Answer these questions, using only short form answers.*

 a Could the writer and his friends hear what the officer said to the Chief Engineer?

 b Had the lifeboat already been lowered into the sea by the time the writer and his friends came up on deck?

 c Was the rescued man carried to ship's hospital?

4 *Complete the following sentences. Your answers must be related to the ideas contained in the passage.*

 a Some of the passengers rushed up on deck before ......

 b The writer and his friends left their table because ......

 c The captain ordered the ship to be turned round so that ......

 d The sailors in the lifeboat began to row as soon as ......

 e The sea was rather rough, so ......

5 *Choose the best explanation according to the context.*

 a *became aware* (1) means

    (i) were frightened   (ii) knew

    (iii) imagined   (iv) decided

6 *Find words or phrases in the passage which mean much the same as the following.*

 a people began to tell one another   b disorder

 c a long time

7 *Composition* Imagine that you were a man in the sea. Describe in not more than 100 words what happened from the time you saw the ship begin to slow down until you were taken on board. Do not include any ideas which are not in the passage. Use your own words as far as possible.

8 In the passage there are several examples of the use of the Passive. Study these and then complete the following sentences by putting the verb in brackets into an appropriate tense in the Passive.

a The man who ...... (*rescue*) had been in the sea for ten hours.

b It always rains when the windows ...... just ...... (*clean*).

c The last time he ...... (*see*) he was wearing a grey suit.

d I'm sure the letter won't arrive in time unless it ...... (*send*) by air.

e It won't be safe to use these stairs until they ...... (*repair*).

f Make sure the door ...... (*lock*) before you go to bed.

g You ...... (*stop*) by a policeman if you try to cross the road now.

h They wouldn't have got ill if the water ...... (*boil*).

i The grass looks as if it ...... (*not, cut*) for years.

j His book fell into the river and ...... (*lose*) for ever.

CICP

20

I left my friend's house shortly after seven. It was still too early for me to have my evening meal, so I walked along the seafront for about an hour until I began to feel hungry. By that time I was not far from a favourite restaurant of mine, where I often went to
5 eat two or three times a week. I knew the owner well and frequently complimented him on his excellent cooking.

I went into the restaurant, which was already crowded, and ordered my meal. While I was waiting for the soup to arrive, I looked around to see if I knew anyone in the restaurant. It was
10 then that I noticed that a man sitting at a corner table near the door kept glancing in my direction, as if he knew me. I certainly did not know him, for I never forget a face. The man had a newspaper open in front of him, which he was pretending to read, though all the while I could see that he was keeping an eye on me. When the
15 waiter brought my soup, the man was clearly puzzled by the familiar way in which the waiter and I addressed each other. He became even more puzzled as time went on and it grew more and more obvious that I was well known in the restaurant. Eventually he got up and went into the kitchen. After a few minutes he came out again, paid
20 his bill and left without another glance in my direction.

When I had finished and was about to pay my bill, I called the owner of the restaurant over and asked him what the man had wanted. The owner was a little embarrassed by my question and at first did not want to tell me. I insisted. "Well," he said, "that man
25 was a detective." "Really?" I said, considerably surprised. "He was certainly very interested in me. But why?" "He followed you here because he thought you were a man he was looking for," the owner of the restaurant said. "When he came into the kitchen, he showed me a photograph of the wanted man. He certainly looked
30 like you! Of course, since we know you here, I was able to convince him that he had made a mistake." "It's lucky I came to a restaurant where I am known," I said, "otherwise I might have been arrested!"

1 *Choose the best answer.*
   a The man at the corner table kept looking at the writer because
      (i) he was bored with reading his newspaper
      (ii) he thought that the writer was someone wanted by the police

(iii) he was afraid that the writer might run away
(iv) he thought he recognised the writer

2 *Answer the following questions briefly, in your own words as far as possible. Use one complete sentence for each answer.*
   a At what time did the writer go to the restaurant?
   b What was the food at the restaurant like?
   c Why was the writer sure that he did not know the man at the corner table?

3 *Answer these questions, using only short form answers.*
   a Did the detective look at the writer after he came out of the kitchen?
   b Had the writer already paid his bill when he called the owner of the restaurant over?
   c Was the detective following the wrong man?

4 *Complete the following sentences. Your answers must be related to the ideas contained in the passage.*

   a The writer walked along the seafront for about an hour because ...
   b The detective was puzzled by the fact that ......
   c The writer insisted that the restaurant owner should tell him ......
   d The detective ......, which he showed to the owner of the restaurant.
   e The detective didn't arrest the writer because ......

5 *Choose the best explanation according to the context.*
   a keeping an eye on (14) means
      (i) watching   (ii) looking at
      (iii) glancing at   (iv) looking in the direction of

6 *Find words or phrases in the passage which mean much the same as the following.*
   a expressed approval of   *b* in the end
   c make someone believe

7 *Composition*   Imagine that you were the detective. Describe in not more than 90 words what happened from the time you followed the man into the restaurant until you paid your bill and left. Do not include any ideas which are not in the passage. Use your own words as far as possible.

58

8 *Notice this sentence:*

He *had* a newspaper *open* in front of him.

In this pattern—verb + direct object + adjective—the adjective is used predicatively and follows the object of the verb. Used in this way, the adjective frequently denotes a state which has been caused by the verbal action.

She opened the cage door and *set* the bird *free*.

Now complete the following sentences with an appropriate verb + adjective from the list given at the foot of the exercise.

a He spoke slowly and emphatically in order to ...... himself ......
b When I opened my suitcase, I ...... it ...... I'd been robbed!
c Don't ...... your eyes ...... by reading too late.
d Three spoonfuls of sugar? You ...... your tea ......!
e Why did they ...... the door ......? I liked the old colour.
f You'll ...... yourself ...... if you eat all those sweets.
g She has six blankets on her bed in winter, but she still can't ...... herself ......
h We've used plenty of soap and hot water, but we still haven't managed to ...... the carpet ......
i You may have to ...... the drawer ...... I think I've lost the key.
j When the dentist tells me to ...... my mouth ......, I always ...... my eyes ...... as well!

break...open	make...clear	paint...red
find...empty	make...sick	shut...tight
keep...warm	make...tired	wash...clean
like...sweet	open...wide	

21

One summer evening I was sitting by the open window, reading a good but rather frightening mystery story. After a time it became too dark for me to read easily, so I put my book down and got up to switch on the light. I was just about to draw the curtains as well
5 when I heard a loud cry of "Help! Help!" It seemed to come from the trees at the end of the garden. I looked out but it was now too dark to see anything clearly. Almost immediately I heard the cry again. It sounded like a child, although I could not imagine how anybody could need help in our garden, unless one of the boys
10 of the neighbourhood had climbed a tree and could not get down.

I decided, however, that I ought to go out and have a look in the garden, just in case someone was in trouble. I took the torch which we keep for going down into the cellar, where there is no electric light, and picked up a strong walking stick, thinking that
15 this might come in useful, too. Armed with these, I went out into the garden. Once again I heard the cry. There was no doubt that it came from the trees at the end of the garden. "Who's there?" I called out as I walked, rather nervously, down the path that led to the trees. But there was no answer. With the help of my torch
20 I examined the whole of that part of the garden and the lower branches of the trees. There was no sign of anybody or anything. I came to the conclusion that someone was playing a rather silly joke on me.

Still feeling rather puzzled, I went back to the house and put
25 away the torch and the stick. I had just sat down and begun to read my book again when I was startled by the cry of "Help! Help!", this time from right behind my shoulder. I dropped my book and jumped up. There, sitting on top of the mantelpiece, was a large green and red bird. It was a parrot! While I was out in the
30 garden, the bird must have seen the light in my room and flown in through the open window.

1 *Give the phrases or sentences in the passage which indicate the following.*
 a The writer did not draw the curtains.
 b The writer had some idea of where the cry of "Help!" came from.
 c The writer used the torch which he took with him into the garden.
 d The writer did not find anyone in the garden.

e The parrot cried "Help!" soon after the writer came back to his room.

2 *Answer the following questions briefly, in your own words as far as possible. Use one complete sentence for each answer.*

a Why did the writer go out into the garden?
b What did the writer arm himself with before he went out?
c Why did the writer think that someone was playing a rather silly joke on him?
d How many times did the writer hear the cry of "Help! Help!"?

3 *Complete the following sentences. Your answers must be related to the ideas contained in the passage.*

a The writer switched on the light because ......
b The writer thought: "Perhaps one of the boys of the neighbourhood ......"
c The writer kept a torch in the house in case ......, where ......
d No sooner ...... than he was startled by the cry of "Help! Help!"
e If the curtains had been drawn, the parrot ......

4 *Explain the meaning of the following words and phrases as they are used in the passage:* neighbourhood (10); in trouble (12); called out (18); examined (20); puzzled (24); startled (26).

5 *Composition* Imagine that you were a friend of the writer of this passage. Write one paragraph, of 120 words, to form part of a longer letter written to a friend, in which you relate the episode of the parrot. Begin your paragraph: "By the way, I must tell you about a very funny thing that happened to a friend of mine the other day." Do not include any ideas which are not in the passage. Use your own words as far as possible.

6 *Notice this sentence:*
It became *too dark for me to read.*
This pattern is made up of too + adjective or adverb + for + (pro)noun + *to*-infinitive. The infinitive expresses consequence. Here is another example:
He ran *too fast for us to catch* him.
Now combine the following pairs of sentences to form one sentence. Follow this model:

61

The window was very small. He could not get through it.
The window was too small for him to get through. (Notice that
it is omitted.)

a The suitcase was very heavy. She couldn't carry it.
b These shoes are very small. I can't wear them.
c The sea was very rough. We couldn't go swimming.
d That ice looks very thin. You can't walk on it.
e He was speaking very quickly. We couldn't catch what he said.
f The postman came very late. We didn't get our letters.
g It's very early. The children can't go to bed yet.
h The soup is very hot. I can't drink it.
i The man was very far away. We couldn't see his face clearly.
j The window was very dirty. No one could see through it.

22

54 Manville Road,
Muswell Hill,
London, N.10.
May 25th, 1983.

5 Dear Mr Ratcliffe,

John Smith is such a common name that I had better remind you
where we met. It was at your daughter's wedding last year. Her
husband David is a very old friend of mine—in fact, we were at
school together—and I came up from London for the occasion. You

10 and I had quite a long chat at the reception and I told you a great
deal about my work as a journalist here in London. You said that
I should get in touch with you if I ever decided to come back to
Durham.

At that time I had every intention of remaining in London, but

15 since then I have changed my mind and I am now very much
inclined to come back to work in my native town. My problem is this:
I have been away now for so long (since 1976, in fact) that I have
very few contacts in Durham. That is why I am writing to you now.
I should really be most grateful if you could put me in touch with

20 anyone who could help or advise me. But please don't put yourself
to a lot of trouble on my behalf. My best wishes to you and your
wife.

Yours sincerely,
John Smith.

25   Haven Villa,
Finch Road,
Durham.
May 29th, 1983.

Dear John,

30   Of course I haven't forgotten you. I remembered who you were as
soon as I saw the signature at the foot of the letter. By a strange
coincidence, my wife and I were talking about you only the other
day. You see, last week I had lunch with a friend of mine who is the
editor of the *Durham Weekly Press*. He was rather worried because

35 he is just about to lose one of his top journalists and so far he has

not been able to find anyone to replace him. He wants someone with wide experience and preferably someone who was born and brought up here. Believe me—and I am not flattering you—I immediately thought of you. I didn't in fact mention your name at the time
40 because last year you seemed so determined to stay in London. My wife thought that I should write to you, just in case you might be interested, but I still hadn't made up my mind to do so when your letter arrived. I rang my friend up at once and he said he would write to you the next day. You may have already heard from him.
45   This is really good news. May I say how glad I am that you have decided to come back to Durham? I look forward very much to meeting you again. My wife and I both send our best wishes.

Yours sincerely,
Bill Ratcliffe.

1 *Give the phrases or sentences in the passage which indicate the following.*
  a John Smith was not sure that Mr Ratcliffe would remember him.
  b John Smith was born in Durham.
  c John Smith did not know many people in Durham who could help him.
  d There was the possibility of a job for John Smith on the *Durham Weekly Press*.
  e Mr Ratcliffe spoke to his friend about John Smith as soon as he got the letter.

2 *Answer the following questions briefly, in your own words as far as possible. Use one complete sentence for each answer.*
  a Why had John Smith been invited to the wedding of Mr Ratcliffe's daughter?
  b How long had John Smith been working in London?
  c What did John Smith ask Mr Ratcliffe to do for him?
  d What kind of journalist was the editor of the *Durham Weekly Press* looking for?

3 *Complete the following sentences. Your answers must be related to the ideas contained in the passage.*
  a "Get in touch with me," Mr Ratcliffe told John Smith, "if ......"
  b John Smith asked Mr Ratcliffe ...... on his behalf.
  c Mr Ratcliffe thought that John wanted to stay in London, so ......
  d As soon as John's letter arrived, ...
  e "......," the editor said, when Mr Ratcliffe rang him up.

4 *Explain the meaning of the following words and phrases as they are used in the passage:* problem (16); on my behalf (21); top (35); wide (37); brought up (37-38); flattering (38).

5 *Composition* Imagine that you were the editor of the *Durham Weekly Press*. Write a brief letter of not more than 100 words to John Smith, mentioning how you had heard his name and inviting him to come to Durham for an interview.

6 *Notice this sentence:*
John Smith is *such* a common name *that I had better remind you . . .*
The clause of result is introduced by *that*, though this is often omitted in spoken English. With an adverb, or when the adjective stands alone, *so* is used instead of *such*:
The name of John Smith is *so common that . . .*

Now combine the following pairs of sentences to form a clause of result, following these models:
It was a wet day. He could not go out.
It was such a wet day (that) he could not go out.
I was tired. I could not walk any further.
I was so tired (that) I could not walk any further.

a The book was dull. Tom couldn't finish it.
b It's a difficult examination. Hardly anyone passes it.
c This is good soup. I think I'll have some more.
d He looked ill. It was hard to recognise him.
e It was a foggy evening. We decided to stay indoors.
f These flowers are cheap. I think I'll buy some more.
g The road is bad. Hardly anyone uses it nowadays.
h He's torn a big hole in his trousers. His mother won't be able to mend them.
i Everybody was quiet. I thought they had all gone to sleep.
j Mary got up late. She nearly missed the train.

23

After a hasty breakfast in the station restaurant, Peter set about the
task of finding a room where he could live for the next few months.
He knew exactly what he wanted: a room which was not too small,
nor so large that it would be difficult to heat in winter. It had to be
5 clean and comfortable too but, above all, it had to be quiet, with a
view that did not look directly on to the street. In the newspaper
he had brought from the bookstall there were very few advertise-
ments for rooms to let. But, as he glanced down the page, a notice
in bold capital letters caught his eye.

10   BOLTON'S ACCOMMODATION AGENCY
                     Flats and Rooms to Let

This seemed promising, so he made a note of the address and set
off in search of the agency. He found it in a narrow street just
off the main road. The woman at the desk gave him a bright smile
15 as he entered and, after he had explained what sort of room he was
looking for, gave him for the small fee of two pounds a list of
about half a dozen landladies who had rooms to let.
At the first house Peter tried, the landlady, who looked about
seventy years old, was so deaf that he had to shout to make her hear.
20 When at last she understood, she shook her head and told him that
she no longer let rooms. At the second house on the list all the
rooms were taken. At the third the landlady was not at home.
Peter was beginning to feel less hopeful, when he noticed that there
was a telephone number after one of the addresses on the list. To
25 save time, therefore, Peter rang up the landlady and enquired if
she had a room to let. He was pleasantly relieved to hear that
she had one vacant. He hurried round to the house, which stood
well back from the road in a pleasant avenue. The room he was
shown lay at the back of the house, overlooking a garden full of
30 flowers and bushes. He noted, too, with satisfaction, that there was a
large table in the room, where he could spread out his books and
work in comfort. Furthermore, the rent was moderate. It was
just what he was looking for. Without hesitation he told the landlady that he would take the room, paid a week's rent in advance
35 and went back to the station to get his luggage.

1 *Give the phrases or sentences in the passage which indicate the following.*
   a Peter did not want a room at the front of the house.
   b He thought that it was worthwhile going to the accommodation agency.
   c The agency was quite near the main road.
   d Peter had to pay for the list of landladies which he got at the agency.
   e There were no rooms vacant at the second house on Peter's list.

2 *Answer the following questions briefly, in your own words as far as possible. Use one complete sentence for each answer.*

   a At what time of day did Peter begin looking for his room?
   b Why did the notice in the newspaper catch his eye?
   c What made Peter begin to lose hope?
   d Why did Peter take the room at the last house without hesitation?

3 *Complete the following sentences. Your answers must be related to the ideas contained in the passage.*

   a Peter had to pay five shillings for ......
   b It was only by shouting that Peter ......
   c Peter saved time by ......
   d When Peter was shown the room, he was pleased to see that ......
   e Peter left his luggage at the station while ......

4 *Explain the meaning of the following words and phrases as they are used in the passage:* above all (5); glanced (8); caught his eye (9); well back (28); overlooking (29); moderate (32).

5 *Composition* Imagine that you were Peter. Describe in not more than 100 words what you did from the time you saw the notice in the newspaper until you reached the fourth house. Do not include any ideas which are not in the passage. Use your own words as far as possible.

6 Notice in these sentences that the defining relative pronoun, the object of the verb, has been omitted:
      In the newspaper [that] Peter had bought ...
      At the first house [that] Peter tried ...
   Compare this with Exercise 6 on page 73.

Now complete the following sentences to form one sentence, omitting the relative pronoun as in the models above. The key word around which the sentence can be built is given for you.

a I bought some red wine. It tasted like ink.
   The red wine ......
b He made a promise. He didn't keep it.
   ...... the promise ......
c You heard a noise. It must have been the wind.
   The noise ......
d I waved to a man just now. He's my bank manager.
   The man ......
e We saw an actor on TV last night. What's his name?
   ...... of the actor ......?
f You lent me a pen. I'm afraid I've lost it.
   ...... the pen ......
g He tells jokes. We don't like them.
   ...... the jokes ......
h You wrote a letter. It never arrived.
   The letter ......
i John sent Mary some flowers. She liked them.
   ...... the flowers ......
j She met a man at a dance. She fell in love with him.
   ...... a man ......

24

Tom was rather looking forward to his first journey by Tube, as the underground railway in London is called. He had heard a great deal about it from his friends who had already been to England. They all advised him not to travel alone the first time. But Tom
5 is the kind of person who never listens to anyone's advice. It is not surprising, therefore, that his first journey by Tube was not a great success.

Tom entered the station shortly after five o'clock in the afternoon. This is a bad time to travel in London, both by bus and
10 train, because crowds of people go home from work at this hour. He had to join a long queue of people who were waiting for tickets. When at last his turn came, he had some difficulty in making the man understand the name of the station he wanted to go to. The people in the queue behind him began to grumble impatiently at the delay.
15 However, he got the right ticket in the end and, by asking several people the way, he also found the right platform. This was packed tight with people. He did not manage to get on the first train, but he was able to move nearer the edge of the platform so as to be in a better position to get on the next one. When this came in,
20 emerging from the tunnel with a terrifying roar, Tom was swept forward on to the train by the rush of people from behind. The doors closed and the train moved off before he was able to get his breath back. He was unable to see the names of the stations where the train stopped, but he had taken the precaution of counting the number of
25 stops so that he knew exactly where to get off. His station was the sixth along the line.

When the train reached the sixth station, Tom got off, feeling relieved that his journey had been so easy. But he was alarmed to see that he had got off at a station that he had never heard of! He
30 did not know what to do. He explained his difficulty to a man who was standing on the platform. With a look of amusement on his face the man told Tom that he had travelled on a train going in the wrong direction.

1 *Give the phrases or sentences in the passage which indicate the following.*
 a It is a waste of time telling Tom what to do.
 b Tom was not the only person who was waiting to buy a ticket.
 c The platform was crowded.
 d The train made a lot of noise as it came out of the tunnel.
 e Tom thought at first that he had arrived at the right station without any difficulty.

2 *Answer the following questions briefly, in your own words as far as possible. Use one complete sentence for each answer.*

 a Why does the writer say that Tom's first journey by Tube was not a great success?
 b Why did the people in the queue behind Tom begin to grumble?
 c How did Tom know where to get off the train?
 d What made Tom realise that he had got off at the wrong station?

3 *Complete the following sentences. Your answers must be related to the ideas contained in the passage.*

 a All Tom's friends advised him: "......"
 b Tom had to ask several people the way in order to ......
 c Tom was in a better position to get on the second train because ......
 d Tom was out of breath when he got on the train because ......
 e "......," the man on the platform told Tom.

4 *Explain the meaning of the following words and phrases as they are used in the passage:* is called (2); shortly (8); queue (11); grumble (14); emerging (20); swept (20).

5 *Composition* Imagine that you were Tom. Write a letter about 100 words long relating what happened to you the first time you travelled by Tube. Do not include any ideas which are not in the passage. Use your own words as far as possible.

6 *Notice how the* to-*infinitive is used in this sentence:*
 He knew exactly *where to get off.*
This means: *where he had to get off.* The *to*-infinitive used after one of the conjunctives *how, where, what, when, whose,* etc., usually contains the idea of obligation or desirability. Here are two more examples:

She didn't know *where to put it* (i.e. where she ought to put it).
He asked us *how to do it* (i.e. the right way to do it).

Now complete the following sentences by selecting a suitable verb from the list given at the foot of the passage.

a Let's ask that policeman over there how ...... the station.
b She's still trying to make up her mind which dress ...... for the party.
c He's lost his pen and doesn't know where ...... it.
d Have you been told which flowers ...... ?
e Keep your eyes closed. I'll tell you when ...... them.
f The boy has climbed on to the roof and doesn't know how ......
g I've been trying to find out where ...... a new umbrella.
h Do you mind telling me how ...... this word?
i She's gone already. No one told her how long ......
j They haven't decided yet whose car ......

buy	open	travel in
get down	pick	wait
get to	pronounce	wear
look for		

25

When I got to the airport, I learnt that the plane from Cairo, on which my brother was travelling, had been delayed at Paris with engine trouble and was expected to be about an hour late. As a rule I can pass the time quite happily, watching the planes
5 land and take off, but that evening I had a headache, which I thought that the noise of the engines might make worse. I decided, therefore, to walk around to make the time pass quickly.

First of all I went back to the place where I had left my car to make sure that all the doors were locked. The walk in the fresh
10 air did me good, for I felt slightly better as I entered the main airport building again. I made my way to the restaurant, where I ordered a cup of black coffee. As I stood drinking this at the counter, I studied the faces of the people around me. Some passengers were obviously anxious about the time, and kept looking at their
15 watches; others checked to see that they had tickets, passports and money. Where there was a group of people, it was easy to tell which one was about to leave. He was the object of everyone's attention and looked either very happy or very sad at the thought of departure. There was one woman who burst into tears as she said
20 goodbye to the relatives or friends who had come to see her off.

When I had finished my coffee, I went along to the bookstall, where I bought a couple of magazines, both of them about travel, which would help to make the time pass pleasantly. Then I went into one of the waiting-rooms and made myself comfortable in a
25 big armchair. I had hardly had time to open one of my magazines when someone came up and put his hand on my shoulder. It was an old friend, who was just about to leave on a business trip to South America. Since we had not seen each other for a long time, we found plenty to talk about until the arrival of my brother's plane
30 from Paris was announced.

1 *Give the phrases or sentences in the passage which indicate the following.*
   a The plane from Cairo had not arrived.
   b The writer usually enjoyed watching the planes land and take off.
   c The writer showed some interest in the people around him in the restaurant.
   d The writer did not have time to read his magazines.
   e The writer's friend had not come to see someone off.

2 *Answer the following questions briefly, in your own words as far as possible. Use one complete sentence for each answer.*

   a Why did the writer go to the airport?

   b Why didn't the writer want to watch the planes landing and taking off?

   c How could you tell, according to the writer, which person in a group was about to leave?

   d Where was the writer when his friend found him?

3 *Complete the following sentences. Your answers must be related to the ideas contained in the passage.*

   a The walk in the fresh air as far as ...... did the writer good.

   b The writer went to the restaurant for ......, which he drank ......

   c You could tell that some people were anxious about the time from the way ......

   d Both the magazines which ...... were about travel.

   e It was a long time since ......, so they had ......

4 *Explain the meaning of the following words and phrases as they are used in the passage:* as a rule (3-4); slightly (10); made my way (11); object of everyone's attention (17-18); to see off (20); old (27).

5 *Composition* Imagine that you had gone to the railway station to meet an old friend arriving from some distant city and found that the train had been delayed. Write a short composition of about 150 words relating some of the things you did to pass the time until your friend's train arrived.

6 In the passage there are some examples of non-defining relative clauses.

   ... I had a headache, which I thought that the noise of the engines might make worse.

Other examples may be found in lines 2, 23 and 27. You should notice that (i) these clauses are always preceded by a comma; (ii) even where the non-defining relative is the object of the verb, it cannot be omitted to form a contact clause.

Compare this with Exercise 6 on page 67.

Now combine the following pairs of sentences to form one sentence, following the model given below.

Mr Smith died last week. He used to live next door to us.

Mr Smith, who used to live next door to us, died last week.

a This book is worth five pounds. I paid only two shillings for it.
b The Liverpool express was late. It should have arrived at 3.15.
c The last speaker made a good speech. He had never spoken in public before.
d He grows a lot of flowers in his garden. He sells most of them.
e This author is now very popular. No one read him twenty years ago.
f I can't understand why Tom doesn't wear glasses. He is very short-sighted.
g His evidence was proved to be false. No one doubted it at the time.
h The lorry crashed into a house. It was carrying a heavy load.
i A distant relative has just left me a lot of money. I never actually met him while he was alive.
j My son starts school in September. He will be five years old next month.

26

The silence of the Reference Library was broken only by an occasional cough and now and then by the scarcely audible sound of pages being turned over. There were about twenty people in the room, most of them with their heads bent over their books. The
5 assistant librarian who was in charge of the room sat at a desk in one corner. She glanced at Phillip as he came in, then went on with her work.

Phillip had not been to this part of the library before. He walked around the room almost on tiptoe, afraid of disturbing the industrious
10 readers with his heavy shoes. The shelves were filled with thick volumes: dictionaries in many languages, encyclopaedias, atlases, biographies and other works of reference. He found nothing that was likely to interest him, until he came to a small section on photography, which was one of his hobbies. The books in this
15 section were on a high shelf out of his reach, so he had to fetch a small ladder in order to get one down. Unfortunately, as he was climbing down the ladder, the book he had chosen slipped from his grasp and fell to the floor with a loud crash. Twenty pairs of eyes looked up at him simultaneously annoyed by this unaccustomed
20 disturbance. Phillip felt himself go red as he picked up his book, which did not seem to have been damaged by its fall.

He had just sat down when he found the young lady assistant standing alongside him. "You must be more careful when you are handling these books," she said severely. Satisfied that she had
25 done her duty, she turned to go back to her desk. Then a sudden thought struck her. "By the way, how old are you?" she asked Phillip. "Thirteen," he told her. "You're not allowed in here under the age of fourteen, you know," the assistant said. "Didn't you see the notice on the door?" Phillip shook his head. He expected the
30 assistant to ask him to leave. Instead, in a more kindly tone, she said: "Well, never mind. But make sure that you don't disturb the other readers again, otherwise I shall have to ask you to leave."

1 *Say whether the following statements are true or false and give the phrases or sentences which indicate this.*
a There was a lot of noise in the Reference Library.
b The assistant did not take much notice of Phillip when he came in.

75

c Phillip knew the Reference Library well.

d Phillip was not interested in photography.

e The assistant nearly forgot to ask Phillip how old he was.

2 *Answer the following questions briefly, in your own words as far as possible. Use one complete sentence for each answer.*

   a How did Phillip try to avoid disturbing the readers in the Reference Library?

   b Where were the books on photography kept?

   c What made Phillip go red?

   d Why did Phillip expect the assistant librarian to ask him to leave?

3 *Complete the following sentences. Your answers must be related to the ideas contained in the passage.*

   a Most of the books on the shelves, such as ......, did not interest Phillip.

   b Phillip would not have disturbed the readers if ......

   c The book ...... was not damaged.

   d The assistant librarian told Phillip severely to ......

   e Phillip did not know that he was too young to use the Reference Library because ......

4 *Explain the meaning of the following words and phrases as they are used in the passage:* scarcely audible (2); industrious (9); atlases (11); grasp (18); simultaneously (19); never mind (31).

5 *Composition* Imagine that you were the assistant librarian. Describe in not more than 90 words what you did and said from the time Phillip dropped the book until you warned him not to disturb the other readers again. Do not include any ideas which are not in the passage. Use your own words as far as possible.

6 *Notice this sentence:*

   Phillip felt himself *go red.*

   In this sentence the verb *go* is followed by an adjective.

   Here are some more examples:

   As we climbed higher, it *became colder.*

   She *looks* remarkably *young.*

   Now complete the following sentences by choosing a suitable verb and adjective from the list given at the foot of the exercise. The verb

76

must also be put into the correct form. Notice which verbs are used in this way.

a It must be quite late. It is already beginning to ......
b John ...... seriously ...... and had to be taken to hospital.
c I'm surprised you ...... * after working so hard.
d The teacher asked the class to ...... while he went out of the classroom.
e I wonder what she's cooking. It certainly ......
f Your daughter ...... much ...... since I last saw her.
g She forgot to put the milk in the refrigerator, so it ......
h Mr Brown had to come back early from his holiday because he ...... of money.
i I didn't recognise him in uniform. He ...... quite ......
j He wanted to be an actor—and now his wish ......

come true	go bad	look different
fall ill	grow taller	run short
feel tired	keep quiet	smell good
get dark		

* Use the negative form.

27

After lunch, without waiting to get permission from their parents, the two boys set off to explore the part of the beach which lay beyond the headland. They persuaded their young sister to stay behind, saying that the long walk would be too tiring for her. Once they 5 had passed beyond the headland, the beach stretched away endlessly in front of them. It was like discovering a new world. And what exciting things there were to do! There were damp, dark caves to explore, in each of which they half expected to come across smugglers hiding; there were innumerable pools among the rocks, 10 full of small fish and other sea-creatures; and, scattered along the beach, there were all those strange, yet commonplace, objects which are washed up and left by the tide.

The afternoon passed quickly and the sun was already beginning to go down when the two boys reluctantly decided to turn back and 15 make their way homewards. Long before they reached the headland, however, they could see that the tide had come in so far that they were now cut off from the other part of the beach. They looked at each other in dismay. It was useless to go on, since clearly there was no way of getting beyond the headland. If, on the other hand 20 they went back the way they had just come, the tide would come in long before they reached the end of the beach. Their only chance of escape was to find a way up the cliff, which in some places was not very steep. At least they might be able to climb high enough to be out of reach of the waves, which were coming closer all the time.

25 In less than ten minutes they found a narrow path which seemed to lead all the way to the cliff top. But their troubles were not yet over. Halfway up, the path was blocked by a large rock, which they could not climb over. The two boys at once began shouting at the 30 top of their voices, hoping that someone walking along the cliff top might hear them. They were both surprised, however, when their father's face appeared over the top of the rock. He told them not to move until he came back. In a short while he reappeared with two policemen, one of whom climbed down a rope which was lowered 35 over the rock. The two boys were then pulled up to safety. At the top of the cliff they found their anxious mother and, with her, their young sister. She had told her parents where they had gone and thus saved them from spending a wet night on the cliff.

1 *Say whether the following statements are true or false and give the phrases or sentences which indicate this.*

    a The boys knew this part of the beach well.
    b The boys did not want to go home.
    c Having considered both going on and turning back, the boys decided that they had to climb the cliff.
    d The boys did not shout very loud.
    e The boys' father climbed down to rescue them.

2 *Answer the following questions briefly, using your own words as far as possible. Use one complete sentence for each answer.*

    a How did the two boys spend their time on the beach?
    b Why did the two boys look at each other in dismay?
    c Why couldn't the two boys get to the top of the cliff?
    d How did their parents know where to look for the two boys?

3 *Complete the following sentences. Your answers must be related to the ideas contained in the passage.*

    a "......," the two boys said to their young sister. "......"
    b While the two boys were exploring the beach beyond the headland, the tide ......
    c "If we go back the way we've just come," the two boys thought, "the tide ......"
    d If the path had not been blocked by a rock, the two boys ......
    e "......," the boys' father told them.

4 *Explain the meaning of the following words and phrases as they are used in the passage:* come across (8); innumerable (9); commonplace (11); closer (24); reappeared (33); anxious (36).

5 *Composition* Imagine that you were one of the boys trapped on the beach. Describe in not more than 100 words what you did from the time you were cut off by the tide until you finally reached the top of the cliff. Do not include any ideas which are not in the passage. Use your own words as far as possible.

6 *Notice this sentence:*
    They *persuaded their young sister to stay behind.*
The sentence pattern here is made up of a verb + direct object (a noun or pronoun) + *to*-infinitive. Here are two more examples:
    The landlady *asked me to pay* a week's rent in advance.
    The teacher *told the class not to make* so much noise.

Now complete the following sentences by (i) supplying a suitable noun or pronoun object; (ii) choosing an appropriate verb from the list given at the foot of the exercise.

a We never expected ...... his temper.
b Perhaps this will help ...... your mind.
c Will you remind ...... the door before I go to bed?
d The Smiths have invited ...... a week-end with them.
e I hope you told ...... our luggage in a first-class compartment.
f Of course you feel sick! We warned ......* all the ice-cream.
g I want ...... these instructions carefully.
h Why did you advise ...... that old car?
i Mrs Roberts has been trying to persuade ...... the garden.
j The teacher didn't allow ...... a dictionary.

buy	lose	read
dig	make up	spend
eat	put	use
lock		

* Use the negative form.

28

The manager waved his hand towards the chair on the other side of the desk and told Henry to take a seat. "I'm waiting for a long-distance call from Manchester," he explained. The telephone rang just as he spoke. The manager picked up the receiver and for some
5 minutes spoke rapidly and impatiently into the telephone. Henry waited, rather regretting that his interview, which he had been dreading for days, had not begun at once. When at last the manager had finished, a secretary came in with a pile of letters. "I really won't keep you waiting much longer," said the manager apologetic-
10 ally, as he picked up the first letter and began to read it. "But these have to catch the next post."

Henry passed the time by examining the manager's office in some detail. On his right there was a large window, heavily curtained, with a view of the factory yard. Henry could see two workmen
15 pushing a trolley across it towards a shed at the far end. Close to the window there were three chairs, arranged around a long, low table, on which stood a jug of water and some glasses. To Henry's left there was a bookcase, which covered the greater part of one wall. The shelves were empty except for a dozen or so reference books, a
20 pile of technical journals, which looked as if they might at any moment slip off the shelf and fall to the ground, and on the top shelf, standing by itself and looking rather out of place in the manager's office, a child's plastic toy. Henry could not help wondering how it came to be there.

25 The most impressive piece of furniture in the room was the manager's desk. Everything on its spacious polished top was arranged with great neatness. On either side of the desk there were two metal trays, one marked IN, the other marked OUT. In the latter tray the manager dropped the letters which he had just signed.
30 Henry had finished his survey of the room when the manager signed the last letter and tossed it into the tray on his right. "That's the lot," he said, as he rang the bell for his secretary to come in and take the letters away. Then he took off his glasses and rubbed his eyes. "Now let me see," he said. "You've come about our
35 advertisement for a clerk in the accounts section, haven't you?"
Henry nodded. His interview had begun.

1 *Say whether the following statements are true or false and give the phrases or sentences which indicate this.*

  a Henry would have liked his interview to begin at once.
  b The secretary waited in the room while the manager signed the letters.
  c The technical journals were very carefully arranged on the top shelf.
  d The manager's desk was very tidy.
  e The manager had no idea what job Henry had come for.

2 *Answer the following questions briefly, in your own words as far as possible. Use one complete sentence for each answer.*

  a How did the manager show Henry where to sit?
  b Why did the manager want to sign the letters before he interviewed Henry?
  c What was happening in the factory yard when Henry looked out of the window?
  d Where did the manager put the letters he had signed?

3 *Complete the following sentences. Your answers must be related to the ideas contained in the passage.*

  a The telephone rang just as the manager was explaining that ......
  b The manager apologised for ......
  c The bookcase was so large that ......
  d ...... because he wanted her to take away the letters which ......
  e Henry nodded when the manager asked him whether ......

4 *Explain the meaning of the following words and phrases as they are used in the passage:* long-distance call (2-3); rapidly (5); dreading (7); reference books (19); spacious (26); latter (29).

5 *Composition* Imagine that you were Henry. Describe in not more than 100 words what you did from the time you came into the room until your interview began. Do not include any ideas which are not in the passage. Use your own words as far as possible.

6 *Notice this sentence:*
  Henry could *see* two men *pushing* a trolley.
  In this pattern the verb of perception (*see, hear, notice,* etc.) is followed by an object (noun or pronoun) + the present participle.

The present participle indicates that we are interested in the continuous nature of the event which is being perceived. Compare this with the pattern used in Exercise 7 on pages 22-3:

Henry *saw* two men *push* the trolley.

Here the interest is in the completed action.

The object + participle pattern is also used with verbs like *find*, *keep* and *catch*, as in lines 8-9:

I won't *keep* you *waiting* much longer.

Now complete the following sentences by choosing a suitable verb from the list given at the foot of the exercise.

a I can hear someone ...... up the stairs.
b We saw several people ...... in the lake.
c I think I can smell something ...... in the kitchen.
d He noticed a letter ...... on the floor just as he was opening the front door.
e The children watched their mother ...... a cake.
f Just look at that cat ... the birds.
g The manager kept Henry ...... until he had finished signing all the letters.
h Can you imagine him ...... the part of Hamlet?
i The librarian caught a boy ...... books from the library.
j I found them already ...... dinner when I arrived.

burn	lie	steal
chase	make	swim
come	play	wait
have		

29

The party began shortly after nine. Mr Wood, who lived in the flat below, sighed to himself as he heard the first signs: the steady tramp of feet on the stairs; the sound of excited voices as the guests greeted one another; and the noise of the gramophone,
5 which was turned full on. Luckily Mr Wood had brought some work home from the office, with which he occupied himself for a couple of hours, thus managing to ignore with some success the party which was going on over his head. But by eleven o'clock he felt tired and was ready to go to bed, though from his experience of
10 previous parties he knew that it was useless trying to get to sleep. He undressed and lay for a while on the bed, trying to read, but the noise from the room directly above his head did not allow him to concentrate on what he was reading. He found himself reading the same page over and over again. He then switched off
15 the light and buried his head in the pillow, in a desperate effort to go to sleep. But even so he could not shut out the noise. Finally, after what seemed hours, he switched on the light and looked at his watch: it was just after midnight.

By now his patience was quite exhausted. He leapt out of bed
20 and, putting a dressing-gown over his pyjamas, marched resolutely up the stairs to his neighbour's flat. He rang the bell several times, but the door remained closed in his face. This did not improve his temper. Just then one of the guests came out and went off down the stairs, leaving the door open. Mr Wood went in. In spite
25 of his odd dress, no one took any notice of him. Then he caught sight of the owner of the flat and managed to attract his attention. The man, whose name was Black, came across the room, smiling cheerfully, and before Mr. Wood could open his mouth to complain, said: "My dear fellow, come in and join us. I know our parties
30 must bother you. I meant to send you an invitation." Mr Wood's ill-humour vanished at once. "I'd better go and get properly dressed," he said. As Mr Wood left the room, Black turned to one of the guests and said: "As soon as I set eyes on him, I knew he'd come to make trouble. That's why I asked him to join us. Did you
35 see how pleased he was? He went off at once to get changed. What a pity the party's nearly over!"

1 *Say whether the following statements are true or false and give the phrases or sentences which indicate this.*

 a The gramophone was very noisy.

 b This was not the first time that there had been a party of this kind in the flat above.

 c Mr Wood did not even try to get to sleep.

 d Mr Wood was angry when he went upstairs to complain.

 e Mr Wood was pleased to be invited to the party.

2 *Answer the following questions briefly, in your own words as far as possible. Use one complete sentence for each answer.*

 a How did Mr Wood manage to ignore the noise of the party until he went to bed?

 b How long had the party been going on when Mr Wood went to complain?

 c In what way was Mr Wood's dress odd?

 d Why did Mr Wood's ill-humour suddenly vanish?

3 *Complete the following sentences. Your answers must be related to the ideas contained in the passage.*

 a The noise from the room directly over Mr Wood's head prevented him ......

 b Although Mr Wood buried his head in the pillow, ...

 c Although Mr Wood rang the doorbell several times, no one ......

 d The guest who came out of the flat ......, so Mr Wood was able to get in.

 e Mr Wood said that ...... before he joined the party.

4 *Explain the meaning of the following words and phrases as they are used in the passage:* steady (2); ignore (7); for a while (11); resolutely (20); bother (30); set eyes on (33).

5 *Composition* Imagine that you were Mr Wood. Describe in not more than 100 words what you did from the time you leapt out of bed until you went back to your flat to change your clothes. Do not include any ideas which are not in the passage. Use your own words as far as possible.

6 *Notice this sentence:*
   By now his patience was *quite* exhausted.

85

Here the meaning of *quite* is *completely*. Compare this with Exercise 7 on page 16, where *quite* = *fairly* or *rather*.

Now complete the following sentences by choosing a suitable word or phrase from the list given at the foot of the exercise. Notice the different ways in which *quite* is used.

a We thought he was going to win the game. We were quite ...... He lost.

b Could you say that again, please? I didn't quite ...... what you said.

c I met Helen the other day quite ......, just as I was getting off the bus.

d This is quite ...... book he has ever written.

e Your translation is not quite ...... There is one small mistake.

f Don't give him any more. He's had quite ...... already.

g Can't you see that they are not the same? They look quite ......

h The noise doesn't disturb me. I'm quite ...... to it.

i Please don't talk so loud. The baby isn't quite ...... yet.

j Are you quite ...... we have come to the right place? You may have made a mistake.

asleep	different	sure
the best	enough	used
by chance	hear	wrong
correct		

30

Mr Price, the antique dealer, lived alone in a small flat above his shop. Because of the many valuable articles which he kept on the premises, he was always afraid that one night someone would break in and rob him. Years before, when he had first come to live
5 there, he had shutters fitted to all the ground-floor windows and strong locks put on all the doors. In addition, he locked up most of his valuable articles in a cupboard, which he had had specially made for this purpose. But, in spite of these precautions, he never felt safe, particularly when he had a lot of money in the flat after a
10 good day's business.

One Saturday night, when he counted his money after closing the shop, he found that he had taken nearly two thousand pounds that day. This was an exceptionally large sum and the thought of keeping it in the house made him feel very nervous. He knew that it
15 would be better to take it to his son's house, where there was a small safe, but it was a foggy evening and his son lived on the other side of town. In the end, he took the money with him to his bedroom, put it in the pocket of one of his overcoats and locked the wardrobe door. He put the key under his pillow and went to bed.

20 Mr Price lay awake for a long time, wondering if his money was really safe, and it was well after midnight before he fell asleep. Almost immediately, or so it seemed, he was woken up by the loud ringing of the shop doorbell. He sat up in bed. Could he have been dreaming? Surely, he thought, no one could want to see him at
25 this hour of the night. The doorbell rang again, echoing through the silent house. He could not help thinking of a story he had read about a man who had been attacked and robbed when he went to answer the door at night. Once again the doorbell rang, more persistently this time.

30 Mr Price got out of bed and went across to the window. The fog had cleared slightly. He opened the window and looked out. He could just make out the shadowy figure of a man standing on the pavement below. "What do you want?" Mr Price called out in a nervous voice. The figure stepped back until it was standing under
35 the street lamp. It was a policeman. "Sorry to disturb you, sir," said the policeman, "but there is a light on in your shop. I think you have forgotten to turn it off."

DICP

87

1 *Say whether the following statements are true or false and give the phrases or sentences which indicate this.*

   a It was not usual for Mr Price to have two hundred pounds in the house after a good day's business.

   b Mr Price locked up the money in his shop.

   c It took Mr Price a long time to get to sleep.

   d Mr Price did not think it was safe to answer the door at night.

   e Mr Price could see the policeman as soon as he looked out of the window.

2 *Answer the following questions briefly, in your own words as far as possible. Use one complete sentence for each answer.*

   a What precautions had Mr Price taken to prevent anyone from breaking into his shop?

   b Why didn't Mr Price take the two hundred pounds to his son's house?

   c How many times did the doorbell ring?

   d Why did the policeman disturb Mr Price?

3 *Complete the following sentences. Your answers must be related to the ideas contained in the passage.*

   a The cupboard in which ...... had been specially made for this purpose.

   b Instead of taking the money to his son's house, Mr Price ......

   c When Mr Price first woke up, he wondered ......

   d Mr Price could not see clearly who was at the door until ......

   e The policeman apologised for ......

4 *Explain the meaning of the following words and phrases as they are used in the passage:* in addition (6); well (21); could not help (26); persistently (29); cleared slightly (31); shadowy (32).

5 *Composition* Imagine that you were the policeman. Describe in about 100 words what you did from the time you saw the light in Mr Price's shop. Relate your account as closely as possible to the ideas contained in the passage.

6 *Notice this sentence:*
   ... (Mr Price) *had shutters fitted* to all the ground floor windows...
Here *have*, with the past participle placed after the object, is used causatively. The meaning of the sentence is that Mr Price did not fit

the shutters himself; he asked (and paid) a man to do it for him. *Get* is also used to express this idea:

He's just gone out to *get his hair cut*.

Now complete the following sentences, paying particular attention to the idea expressed.

a I'm going to have my eyes ...... (*test*) tomorrow.
b Your handwriting is difficult to read. You ought to have your letters ...... (*type*).
c Those trousers don't fit you. Why don't you get them ...... (*alter*)?
d What a pity she has had her hair ...... (*dye*).
e I used to have this newspaper ...... (*send*) to me while I was abroad.
f The tree in the front garden makes the room dark. We ought to get it ...... (*cut down*).
g This room will look a lot better when we get this old fireplace ...... (*take out*) and a new one ...... (*put in*).
h Leave these suitcases in the hall and I'll have them ...... (*send up*) to your room later.
i How much does it cost to have a suit ...... (*clean*)?
j These are the photographs we had ...... (*take*) at the wedding.

Section two
Recall Exercises

Verbs

Complete each of the following passages by supplying the correct form of the verb.

(a) That evening I ...... (*go*) ...... (*have*) dinner with an uncle and aunt of mine. They ...... also ...... (*invite*) another person, a young woman, so that there ...... (*be*) four people at table. The young woman's face ...... (*be*) familiar, but I ...... (*not, can*) ...... (*remember*) where I ...... (*see*) it. I ...... (*be*) quite sure that we ...... (*not, meet*) before. In the course of conversation, however, the young woman ...... (*happen*) ...... (*remark*) that she ...... (*lose*) her purse that afternoon. I at once ...... (*remember*) where I ...... (*see*) her face. She ...... (*be*) the young girl in the photograph, although she ...... (*be*) now much older. Of course she ...... (*be*) very surprised when I ...... (*be able*) ...... (*describe*) her purse to her. Then I ...... (*explain*) that I ...... (*recognise*) her face from the photograph I ...... (*find*) in the purse. (*CP2*)

(b) The children ...... (*stop*) ...... (*chatter*) as Miss Hughes ...... (*enter*) the classroom. Then they ...... (*stand up*) as one body and ...... (*say*) in a loud chorus:
   "Good morning, teacher."
   Miss Hughes ...... (*smile*), ... (*say*) good morning too and ...... (*tell*) the class ...... (*sit down*). At a glance there ...... (*seem*) ...... (*be*) about thirty-five pupils in the class. The majority ...... (*be*) girls. She ...... (*notice*) several intelligent faces. All the pupils ...... (*watch*) her intently, ... (*wait*) no doubt ...... (*find out*) what sort of a person she ...... (*be*).
   "I ...... (*suppose*) you ...... (*want*) ...... (*know*) my name," she ...... (*say*). But before she ...... (*can*) ...... (*tell*) them, someone in the class ...... (*call out*): "It ...... (*be*) Miss Hughes." Everyone ...... (*laugh*). Miss Hughes ...... (*laugh*) too. (*CP5*)

(c) Helen ...... (*be*) now quite sure that she ...... (*be going*) ...... (*miss*) her train, although she ...... (*be*) not very far from the station. She ...... (*wonder*) what ...... (*do*) when a bus ...... (*come*) into sight, ... (*go*) in the direction of the station. The bus stop ...... (*be*) not far off, so Helen ...... (*get*) her suitcase out of the taxi and ...... (*run*) towards the bus, which ...... (*stop*) ...... (*let*) some passengers ...... (*get off*). The bus conductor ...... (*see*) her ...... (*run*) and ...... (*not, ring*) the bell for the bus ...... (*start*) until she ...... (*get on*). Helen ...... (*reach*) the station just in time and ...... (*manage*) ...... (*catch*) her train after all. But if she ...... (*wait for*) the taxi driver ...... (*stop*) ...... (*argue*), she ...... probably ...... (*miss*) it.   (*CP7*)

(*d*) "I ...... (*wish*) he ...... (*let*) me ...... (*know*)," the young man ...... (*say*). "I ...... (*write*) him a letter ...... (*sa ʹ*) that I ...... (*come*). I ...... (*have*) all this trouble for nothing. Well, since he ...... (*not, be*) here, there ...... (*be*) no point in ...... (*wait*)."

He ...... (*thank*) Mrs Crump and ...... (*go out*). Mrs Crump ...... (*go*) to the window and ...... (*watch*) him ...... (*drive off*). When his car ...... (*be*) out of sight, she ...... (*call out*):

"You ...... (*can*) ...... (*come out*) now, Mr White. He ...... (*go*)."

Mr White ...... (*come out of*) the kitchen, where he ...... (*wait*).

"Many thanks, Mrs Crump," he ...... (*say*) ...... (*laugh*). "You ...... (*do*) that very well. These nephews of mine never ...... (*give*) me any peace. That young man ...... (*be*) the worst of them all. As you ...... (*see*), when he ...... (*need*) money, he even ...... (*follow*) me into the country. Well, perhaps next time he ...... (*not, warn*) me by ...... (*write*) me a letter!"   (*CP8*)

(*e*) I ...... (*be*) delighted ...... (*get*) your letter this morning. I really ought ...... (*write*) to you—it ...... (*be*) my turn, I ...... (*know*)—but I ...... (*be*) terribly busy. The children ...... (*seem*) ...... (*take up*) all my time. I ...... (*think*) of ...... (*send*) Ann to a nursery school. She ...... (*be*) four next month. Baby ...... just ...... (*start*) ...... (*walk*) and ...... (*not, give*) me a moment's peace. But you ...... (*know*) what it ...... (*be*) like! How ...... (*be*) all your children? I ...... (*be*) sure they ...... (*love*) ...... (*live*) in the country.

I ...... (*be*) afraid we ...... (*not, can*) ...... (*come over*) ...... (*see*) you next Sunday, as you ...... (*suggest*). Tom's mother ...... (*come*) ...... (*spend*) the day with us. What about the Sunday after that—the twenty-second? We ...... (*be*) free that day and ...... (*love*) ...... (*come*). We ...... (*long*) ...... (*see*) your new house.   (*CP9*)

(*f*) "Oh! I ...... (*be*) stupid!" ...... (*say*) Mrs Brown. "I ...... (*leave*) all my shopping in the restaurant and now I ...... (*be*) lost."

She ...... still ...... (*wonder*) what ...... (*do*) when a policeman ......

(*come up*) and ...... (*ask*) if he ...... (*can*) ...... (*help*). Mrs Brown ......
(*explain*) what ...... (*happen*).

"Well, first of all," ...... (*say*) the policeman, "we ...... (*have*) better
...... (*go back*) as far as the chemist's."

"Now," ...... (*suggest*) the policeman, when they ...... (*get to*) the
chemist's, "let's ...... (*go*) in this direction. It ...... (*lead*) to the main
road, where we ...... probably ...... (*find*) your restaurant."

When they ...... (*reach*) the main road, the policeman ...... (*say*):

"I ...... (*think*) you ...... (*find*) the restaurant you ...... (*look for*)
along there, on the opposite side of the road."   (*CP11*)

(g) "You ...... (*buy*) old books, don't you ?" ...... (*ask*) Fred, ... (*put*)
his parcel down on the shop counter.

"I ...... (*have to*) ...... (*see*) what you ∴..... (*get*) before I ...... (*can*)
...... (*answer*) that question," the bookseller ...... (*say*). "Business ......
(*not, be*) so good as it used ...... (*be*). People ...... (*seem*) ...... (*prefer*) ......
(*buy*) new books nowadays."

Fred ...... (*open*) his parcel and ...... (*lay*) the books out on the
counter.

"I ...... (*not, pretend*) ...... (*know*) much about books," he ...... (*say*).
"I ...... (*have*) these for years and I ...... even ...... (*not, read*) them.
My grandfather ...... (*leave*) them to me, as a matter of fact. But my
wife never ...... (*stop*) ...... (*complain*) about them. She ...... (*say*) they
...... (*make*) the place ...... (*look*) dirty. So I ...... (*think*) I ...... (*bring*)
them in ...... (*show*) you, just in case there ...... (*be*) anything of
interest."   (*CP13*)

(h) It ......∴. (*be*) dark in the attic, as Miss Manning ...... (*warn*) him.
Weston ...... (*find*) the small window in the roof and ...... (*force*) it
open, thus ...... (*let in*) more light. He ...... (*can*) just ...... (*make out*)
the boxes which Miss Manning ...... (*tell*) him about.

"When my father ...... (*die*)," Miss Manning ...... (*say*), "his large
library ...... (*sell up*). His papers, and some other possessions of no
great value, ... (*store*) in boxes and ...... (*put up*) in the attic. They
...... (*be*) there ever since. I ...... (*not, suppose*) the room ...... (*open*)
for over ten years."

"What about his diaries ?" ...... (*ask*) Weston. "In one of his letters
to a friend, Colonel Manning ...... (*mention*) that he ...... (*keep*) a
diary."

"I ...... (*not, remember*) ...... (*see*) any diaries," ...... (*say*) Miss

92

Manning, with a puzzled look on her face. "Of course he may ......
(*destroy*) them before his last illness. Otherwise they ...... (*must*) ......
(*be*) in those boxes in the attic."

(*i*) On May 1st we ...... (*plan*) ...... (*hold*) a dinner ...... (*celebrate*)
the fifth anniversary of the Selmore Literary Society and I ...... (*ask*)
by our committee ...... (*invite*) you ...... (*be*) the guest of honour on this
occasion. Since you ...... (*come*) ...... (*live*) in our town last year, you
...... always ...... (*show*) a great deal of interest in our activities and you
...... (*be*) without doubt our most popular speaker. We ...... all ...... (*be*)
delighted as well as highly honoured if you ...... (*can*) once again ......
(*find*) the time ...... (*spend*) an evening in our company. I ...... (*send*)
you further details as soon as I ...... (*hear*) from you. I ...... (*hope*)
you ...... (*be able*) ...... (*accept*) this invitation. (*CP16*)

(*j*) "Now, sir," ...... (*say*) Inspector Robinson, ... a chair ......
(*draw up*) close to the injured man's bed and ...... (*sit down*), "I ......
(*hope*) you ...... (*feel*) well enough ...... (*answer*) a few questions."
"Yes, of course," ...... (*say*) Topham. He ...... (*sit up*) in bed. The
nurse ...... (*place*) another pillow behind his head and ...... (*leave*) the
room.
"First of all," ...... (*say*) the inspector, ... (*open*) his notebook,
"we ...... (*have to*) ...... (*establish*) your identity."
Topham ...... (*look*) astonished. "My identity? ...... you even ......
(*not, know*) who I ...... (*be*)? How long ...... I ...... (*lie*) in hospital?"
"Three days," the inspector ...... (*tell*) him. "But we ...... (*find*)
no papers on you at all. Whoever ...... (*attack*) you also ...... (*steal*)
your wallet."
"But what about my car?" ...... (*ask*) Topham. "Surely you could
...... (*find out*) my identity from that?"
"Your car ...... (*steal*) too," the inspector ...... (*explain*) patiently.
"So, you ...... (*see*), we ...... (*be*) completely in the dark." (*CP18*)

(*k*) We first ...... (*become*) aware that something unusual ...... (*happen*)
when one of the ship's officers ...... (*come*) up to the Chief Engineer,
who ...... (*sit*) at our table, and ...... (*speak*) to him in a low voice. The
Chief Engineer at once ...... (*stand up*) and with a brief excuse, which
...... (*tell*) us nothing, ... (*leave*) the dining-room. At first we ......
(*think*) that there ...... (*be*) an accident or that a fire ...... (*break out*)
on board ship, but soon the word ...... (*go round*) that a man ...... (*see*)

93

...... (*float*) in the sea. Then we ...... (*notice*) that the ship ...... (*slow down*) and ...... (*begin*) ...... (*turn round*) with rather a violent motion. Some of the passengers ...... (*not, wait*) ...... (*finish*) their meal, but at once ...... (*rush*) up on deck. Others ...... (*crowd*) round the portholes, ... (*make*) it impossible for us ...... (*eat*) in comfort. There ...... (*be*) such confusion in the dining-room that we ...... (*decide*) ...... (*join*) those who ...... (*go*) up on deck. (*CP19*)

(*l*) When I ...... (*finish*) my meal and ...... (*be*) about ...... (*pay*) my bill, I ...... (*call*) the owner of the restaurant over and ...... (*ask*) him what the man ...... (*want*). The owner ...... (*be*) a little embarrassed by my question and at first ...... (*not, want*) ...... (*tell*) me. I ...... (*insist*). "Well," he ...... (*say*), "that man ...... (*be*) a detective." "Really?" I ...... (*say*), considerably surprised. "He ...... (*be*) certainly very interested in me. But why?" "He ...... (*follow*) you here because he ...... (*think*) you ...... (*be*) a man he ...... (*look for*)," the owner of the restaurant ...... (*say*). "When he ...... (*come*) into the kitchen, he ...... (*show*) me a photograph of the wanted man. He certainly ...... (*look*) like you! Of course, since we ...... (*know*) you here, I ...... (*be able*) ...... (*convince*) him that he ...... (*made*) a mistake." "It ...... (*be*) lucky I ...... (*come*) to a restaurant where I ...... (*know*), " I ...... (*say*), "otherwise I might ...... (*arrest*)!" (*CP20*)

(*m*) At that time I ...... (*have*) every intention of ...... (*remain*) in London, but since then I ...... (*change*) my mind and I ...... (*be*) now very much inclined ...... (*come back*) ...... (*work*) in my native town. My problem ...... (*be*) this: I ...... (*be*) away now for so long (since 1956, in fact) that I ...... (*have*) very few contacts in Durham. That ...... (*be*) why I ...... (*write*) to you now. I should really ...... (*be*) most grateful if you ...... (*can*) ...... (*put*) me in touch with anyone who ...... (*can*) ...... (*help*) or ...... (*advise*) me. But please ...... (*not, put*) yourself to a lot of trouble on my behalf. (*CP22*)

(*n*) He ...... just ...... (*sit down*) when he ...... (*find*) the young lady assistant ...... (*stand*) alongside him. "You must ...... (*be*) more careful when you ...... (*handle*) these books," she ...... (*say*) severely. Satisfied that she ...... (*do*) her duty, she ...... (*turn*) ...... (*go back*) to her desk. Then a sudden thought ...... (*strike*) her. "By the way, how old ...... (*be*) you?" she ...... (*ask*) Phillip. "Thirteen," he ...... (*tell*) he "You ...... (*not, allow*) in here under the age of fourteen, you ...... (*know*),"

the assistant ...... (*say*). "...... you ...... (*not, see*) the notice on the
door?" Phillip ...... (*shake*) his head. He ...... (*expect*) the assistant
...... (*ask*) him ...... (*leave*). Instead, in a more kindly tone, she ......
(*say*): "Well, never...... (*mind*). But ...... (*make*) sure that you ......
(*not, disturb*) the other readers again, otherwise I ...... (*have to*) ......
(*ask*) you ...... (*leave*).   (*CP26*)

(*o*) The manager ...... (*wave*) his hand towards the chair on the other
side of the desk and ...... (*tell*) Henry ...... (*take*) a seat. "I ...... (*wait
for*) a long-distance call from Manchester," he ...... (*explain*). The
telephone ...... (*ring*) just as he ...... (*speak*). The manager ...... (*pick
up*) the receiver and for some time ...... (*speak*) rapidly and impatiently
into the telephone. Henry ...... (*wait*), rather ...... (*regret*) that his
interview, which he ...... (*dread*) for days, ... (*not, begin*) at once.
When at last the manager ...... (*finish*), a secretary ...... (*come in*) with
a pile of letters. "I really ...... (*not, keep*) you ...... (*wait*) much longer,"
...... (*say*) the manager apologetically, as he ...... (*pick up*) the first
letter and ...... (*begin*) ...... (*read*) it. "But these ...... (*have to*) ......
(*catch*) the next post."   (*CP28*)

Articles

Complete each of the following passages by supplying *a, an* or *the*.

(*a*) While I was walking along ...... road ...... other day, I happened to notice ...... small brown leather purse lying on ...... pavement. I picked it up and opened it to see if I could find out ...... owner's name. There was nothing inside it except some small change and ...... rather old photograph—......picture of ...... woman and ...... young girl about twelve years old, who looked like ...... woman's daughter. I put ...... photograph back and took ...... purse to ...... police station, where I handed it to ...... sergeant in charge. Before I left, ... sergeant made ...... note of my name and address in case ...... owner of ...... purse wanted to write and thank me. (*CP2*)

(*b*) It was time to start ...... lesson. "Now let me see," said Miss Hughes, looking at ...... timetable. "...... first lesson is English."

"Oh, please, tell us ...... story," begged one of ...... girls.

Several of ...... pupils repeated this. Miss Hughes smiled.

"Very well," she said. "But first of all I want you to write ...... letter to John Young. We'll send ...... best ones to cheer him up in hospital. Afterwards I'll tell you ...... story, if you're good."

They were all writing busily when Miss Hughes slipped out of ...... classroom to fetch ...... book which she had left in ...... staffroom. She passed ...... headmistress in ...... corridor.

"Any trouble from that class?" asked ...... headmistress.

"Not so far," said Miss Hughes confidently. "They all seem very well behaved." (*CP5*)

(*c*) Just then he noticed that her bottle of milk, which was delivered early in ...... morning, was still on ...... doorstep. This worried him. If Mrs Dunley had not taken in her milk, perhaps she was ill. Bill walked round ...... house until he found ...... open window. It was small but he just managed to squeeze through. He went into ...... hall. There he almost fell over Mrs Dunley, who was lying at ...... foot of ...... stairs, unconscious. Realising that there was little he could do for her, Bill rushed out of ...... house, stopped ...... passing car and told ...... driver to telephone for ...... ambulance as soon as he got to ...... village. (*CP6*)

(*d*) Just then ...... taxi came slowly down ...... road. Helen knew

96

that ...... fare to ...... station was at least five shillings, which was more than she could afford; but she quickly made up her mind that it would be well worth ...... extra expense in order to be sure of catching her train. So she stopped ...... taxi and got in. She told ...... driver that she had to catch ...... train which left at half past two. ...... man nodded and said that he would take ...... short cut to get her to ...... station in good time. (*CP7*)

(*e*) He was just in ...... middle of describing ...... rather terrifying experience he had once had when his small sailing boat was carried out to sea in ...... storm, when there was ...... loud crash from ...... bedroom above, ... one where my brother and I were going to sleep.

"It sounds as if ...... roof has fallen in!" exclaimed my uncle, with ...... loud laugh.

When we got to ...... top of ...... stairs and opened ...... bedroom door, we could see nothing at first because of ...... thick clouds of dust which filled ...... room. When these began to clear, ... strange sight met our eyes. ...... large part of ...... ceiling had collapsed, falling right on to ...... pillow of my bed. (*CP10*)

(*f*) When he saw ...... last book, however, his eyes lit up with excitement.

"What is it?" asked Fred.

"Now this *is* worth something," exclaimed ...... bookseller, turning over ...... pages. "It's ...... very rare edition."

He handed ...... book to Fred, who looked at ...... title. It was ...... novel of ...... last century by ...... author whose name he had never heard of. Of all ...... books he had gathered together to bring to ...... bookshop, this one had looked ...... least interesting. (*CP13*)

(*g*) After searching through ...... number of drawers, Miss Manning found ...... key to ...... attic.

"You won't find it easy to see up there," she said as she handed him ...... key. "There's ...... small window in ...... roof but I expect that it will be too dirty to see through."

There were about ...... dozen boxes in all. Weston did not know where to begin. He opened first one, then ...... other, but he found nothing that looked like diaries. Then he decided to try ...... largest box. It was full of papers. As he turned these over, ... bundle of exercise books, tied together with string, caught his eye. On ...... cover of ...... top one were written ...... words "DIARY, 1935-36". (*CP15*) (*h*) ...... small crowd had gathered round ...... entrance to ...... park. His curiosity aroused, Robert crossed ...... road to see what was happening. He found that ...... centre of attraction was ...... old man with ...... performing monkey: ...... monkey's tricks were in no way remarkable so, after throwing ...... few pennies in ...... dirty hat which ...... man had placed on ...... pavement, Robert began to move off, along with other members of ...... crowd.   (*CP17*)

(*i*) ...... few months later, Robert came across ...... old man again in another part of ...... city. ...... man had ...... new monkey, bought no doubt with ...... money which ...... crowd had given him. It did not, however, seem any better at its tricks than ...... previous one. Robert was pleased to see that ...... old man was still able to earn ...... living, though on this occasion, having partly paid for ...... monkey out of his own pocket, he did not feel inclined to throw any money into ...... hat.   (*CP17*)

(*j*) There we learnt that one of ...... crew had seen ...... man in ...... sea some distance from ...... ship. He had informed ...... captain, who at once ordered ...... ship to be turned round. We were now only two hundred yards or so from ...... man, and ...... lifeboat had already been lowered into ...... sea. In it there were four sailors, who were sitting ready at ...... oars, ... officer and ...... ship's doctor. ...... officer shouted ...... order and ...... sailors began to row away from ...... ship. By looking in ...... same direction as ...... boat was going, we were able to make out ...... position of ...... man in ...... water. He was clinging to ...... large piece of wood.   (*CP19*)

(*k*) I decided, however, that I ought to go out and have ...... look in ...... garden, just in case someone was in trouble. I took ...... torch which we keep for going down into ...... cellar, where there is no electric light, and picked up ...... strong walking stick, thinking that this might come in useful, too. Armed with these, I went out into ...... garden. Once again I heard ...... cry. There was no doubt that it came from ...... trees at ...... end of ...... garden. "Who's there?" I called out as I walked, rather nervously, down ...... path that led to ...... trees. But there was no answer. With ...... help of my torch, I examined ...... whole of that part of ...... garden and ...... lower branches of ...... trees. There was no sign of anybody or anything. I came to ...... conclusion that someone was playing ...... rather silly joke on me.

(*CP21*)

(*l*) Peter was beginning to feel less hopeful when he noticed that there was ...... telephone number after one of ...... addresses on ...... list. To save time, therefore, Peter rang up ...... landlady and enquired if she had ...... room to let. He was pleasantly relieved to hear that she had one vacant. He hurried round to ...... house, which stood well back from ...... road in ...... pleasant avenue. ...... room he was shown lay at ...... back of ...... house, overlooking ...... garden full of flowers and bushes. He noted, too, with satisfaction, that there was ...... large table in ...... room, where he could spread out his books and work in comfort. Furthermore, ... rent was moderate. It was just what he was looking for. Without hesitation he told ...... landlady that he would take ...... room, paid ...... week's rent in advance and went back to ...... station to get his luggage. (*CP23*)

(*m*) When I had finished my coffee, I went along to ...... bookstall, where I bought ...... couple of magazines, both of them about travel, which would help make ...... time pass pleasantly. Then I went into one of ...... waiting-rooms and made myself comfortable in ...... big armchair. I had hardly had time to open one of my magazines when someone came up and put his hand on my shoulder. It was ...... old friend, who was just about to leave on ...... business trip to South America. Since we had not seen each other for ...... long time, we found plenty to talk about until ...... arrival of my brother's plane from Paris was announced. (*CP25*)

(*n*) Henry passed ...... time by examining ...... manager's office in some detail. On his right there was ...... large window, heavily curtained, with ...... view of ...... factory yard. Henry could see two workmen pushing ...... trolley across it towards ...... shed at ...... far end. Close to ...... window there were three chairs, arranged around ...... long, low table, on which stood ...... jug of water and some glasses. To Henry's left there was ...... bookcase, which covered ...... greater part of one wall. ...... shelves were empty except for ...... dozen or so reference books, ... pile of technical journals, which looked as if they might at any moment slip off ...... shelf and fall to ...... ground, and on ...... top shelf, standing by itself and looking rather out of place in ...... manager's office, ... child's plastic toy. (*CP28*)

(*o*) Mr Price, ... antique dealer, lived alone in ...... small flat above his shop. Because of ...... many valuable articles which he kept on ...... premises, he was always afraid that one night someone would break in

99

and rob him. Years before, when he had first come to live there, he had shutters fitted to all ...... ground floor windows and strong locks put on all ...... doors. In addition, he locked up most of his valuable articles in ...... cupboard, which he had had specially made for this purpose. But, in spite of these precautions, he never felt safe, particularly when he had ...... lot of money in ...... flat after ...... good day's business.

(*CP30*)

Prepositions and Adverbial Particles

Complete each of the following passages by supplying the correct preposition or adverbial particle.

(a) It was already late when we set .... the next town, which .... the map was about fifteen miles away ...... the other side ...... the hills. There we felt sure we would find a bed ...... the night. Darkness fell soon after we left the village but luckily we met no one as we drove swiftly ...... the narrow winding road that led ...... the hills. As we climbed higher, it became colder and rain began to fall, making it difficult ...... times to see the road. I asked John, my companion, to drive more slowly.

After we had travelled ...... about twenty miles, there was still no sign ...... the town which was marked ...... the map. We were beginning to get worried. Then, ..,.... warning, the car stopped. A quick examination showed that we had run .... petrol. Although we had little food ...... us, only a few biscuits and some chocolate, we decided to spend the night ...... the car.   (CP1)

(b) Then there is a man I do not care ...... very much, an engineer ...... the name ...... Barlow. He has been ...... leave ...... England and is now returning ...... his work ...... Singapore. He seems full ...... energy: he swims or plays tennis the best part ...... the day. I have never ...... my life met a man ...... such a loud laugh. He has the cabin .... mine and I can hear his laugh even ...... the wall!

The other person who sits ...... our table is Mrs Hunt. I have found ...... hardly anything ...... her. She is extremely quiet and rarely talks except to consult the doctor ...... her children's ailments. She is ...... her way to join her husband ...... India.   (CP3)

(c) Half an hour ...... daybreak three ...... the boys assembled, as they had agreed, ... the old bridge. The fourth, a boy ...... the name ...... ᴛolly, had not turned ...... His absence did not greatly surprise the others. They knew that his mother did not want him to come ...... this expedition ...... the forest.

Charles, who was the oldest and their accepted leader, waded downstream ...... the place where the boat was tied .... the shelter ...... some overhanging bushes. Then he rowed the boat .... the shallow water ...... the bridge, where the boys loaded it ...... provisions, blankets and other things which they were taking ...... their journey.   (CP4)

101

(d) Bill Fuller, the postman, whistled cheerfully as he pushed his bicycle ...... the hill ...... old Mrs Dunley's house. His work ...... the day was almost finished; his bag, usually quite full when he set .... his round, was empty now .... the letter that he had to deliver ...... Mrs Dunley. She lived ...... a mile ...... the village so that, when Bill had a letter ...... her, he always finished his day's work much later. He did not mind this, however, because she never failed to ask him .... a cup ...... tea.   (CP6)

(e) A car drew .... the Swan Hotel and a young man got ...... Pausing only ...... an instant to see that he had come ...... the right place, he went ...... the hotel and rang the bell ...... the counter ...... the bar.

Mrs Crump, the landlady, who was busy ...... the kitchen ...... the time, hurried ......, wiping her hands. The young man raised his hat.

"Excuse me," he said. "I'm looking ...... my uncle, Mr White. I believe he is staying here."

"He *was* staying here," Mrs Crump corrected him. "But I'm afraid he went .... London yesterday."

"Oh, dear," said the young man, looking disappointed. I understood that he was going to stay here ...... the end ...... the month. ...... least, that is what his servant told me when I rang ...... his house."   (CP8)

(f) Mrs Brown was tired ...... her day's shopping ...... London, so she went ...... a restaurant ...... a cup ...... tea ...... catching the train home. When she had ordered her tea, she suddenly remembered that she had to buy some medicine ...... her husband, who had a bad cough.

"Is there a chemist's ...... here?" she asked the waiter.

"Yes, madam," the waiter said, "it's only about three minutes' walk ...... Turn right when you go .... the restaurant, then take the second turning ...... the left. You'll find a big chemist's about a hundred yards ...... the road ...... the right-hand side. It closes ...... five but if you hurry, you'll just get there ...... time."

Mrs Brown followed the waiter's directions carefully and found the chemist's shop ...... any difficulty. She bought the cough mixture and started to make her way .... the restaurant. But after she had walked ...... about ten minutes and there was still no sign ...... the restaurant, she realised that she must have made a mistake.   (CP11)

(g) Luckily ...... that moment he was much too busy talking ...... the

102

man opposite him to catch sight ...... me. I slipped .... my compartment, took ...... my two suitcases and carried them ...... the far end ...... the corridor so as to be ready to get ...... the train as soon as it stopped. The moment the train came ...... a halt, I called a porter, who ...... no time ...... all had carried my luggage .... the station and found me a taxi. As I drove ...... my small hotel ...... the outskirts ...... the town, I breathed a deep sigh ...... relief ...... my narrow escape. There was little chance that I should run ...... my boring ex-neighbour again. (*CP12*)

(*h*) Then one ...... the men looked ...... his watch, clapped his hands and said something ...... the others. Immediately they all went ...... their desks and, ... the space ...... a few seconds, everyone was working busily. No one took any notice ...... Mary ...... all. ...... last she went .... the man who was sitting ...... the desk nearest the door and explained that this was her first day ...... the office. Hardly looking .... his work, he told her to take a seat ...... him and wait ...... Mr King, who would arrive ...... any moment. Then Mary realised that the day's work ...... the office began just before Mr King arrived. Later she found ...... that he came ...... every morning ...... the country ...... the same train, arriving promptly ...... the office ...... 9.35, so that his staff knew precisely when to start work. (*CP14*)

(*i*) Thank you ...... your letter ...... April 7th, which I am answering ...... behalf ...... my husband. Apparently you have not heard that about a month ago my husband was taken seriously ill, as a result ...... overwork. Although he is now much better, the doctor has ordered him to take a complete rest .... least three months. As a matter ...... fact we are leaving ...... the continent as soon as he is fit to travel and it is unlikely that we shall return ...... England ...... the end ...... July.
...... view ...... this, I regret that my husband is unable to accept this kind invitation ...... the dinner which your society is holding ...... May 1st. He has asked me, however, to send his very best wishes ...... the success ...... the occasion and says that he hopes to be ...... you again ...... the autumn. (*CP16*)

(*j*) "I'm a widower," Topham said. "I've lived alone ever since my wife died three years ago. This year, as always, I went to spend my holidays ...... the sea. I decided to come ...... early .... the bad weather. ...... my way .... London I stopped ...... the Sun Inn ...... dinner."

The inspector nodded and waited ...... Topham to go ......

"It was raining pretty hard when I came .... the hotel. I dashed ...... the car park, where I had left my car. I had just unlocked the door and was getting ...... when a man stepped .... the shadows and asked me ...... a lift ...... London. Before I had time to reply, he attacked me. ...... that I can remember nothing until I woke .... hospital. (CP18)

(k) Still feeling rather puzzled, I went .... the house and put ...... the torch and the stick. I had just sat ...... and begun to read my book again when I was startled ...... the cry ...... "Help! Help!", this time ...... right ...... my shoulder. I dropped my book and jumped ...... There, sitting ...... top ...... the mantelpiece, was a large green and red bird. It was a parrot! While I was .... the garden, the bird must have seen the light ...... my room and flown .... the open window. (CP21)

(l) Tom entered the station shortly ...... five o'clock ...... the afternoon. This is a bad time to travel ...... London, both ...... bus and train, because crowds ...... people go home ...... work ...... this hour. He had to join a long queue ...... people who were waiting ...... tickets. When ...... last his turn came, he had some difficulty ...... making the man understand the name ...... the station he wanted to go ...... The people ...... queue ...... him began to grumble impatiently ...... the delay. However, he got the right ticket ...... the end and, ... asking several people the way, he also found the right platform. This was packed tight ...... people. He did not manage to get ...... the first train, but he was able to move nearer the edge ...... the platform so as to be ...... a better position to get ...... the next one. (CP24)

(m) ...... lunch, ... waiting to get permission ...... their parents, the two boys set ...... to explore the part ...... the beach which lay ...... the headland. They persuaded their young sister to stay ......, saying that the long walk would be too tiring ...... her. Once they had passed ...... the headland, the beach stretched ...... endlessly ...... front ...... them. It was like discovering a new world. And what exciting things there were to do! There were damp, dark caves to explore, ... each ...... which they half expected to come ...... smugglers hiding; there were innumerable pools ...... the rocks, full ...... small fish and other sea-creatures; and, scattered ...... the beach, there were all those strange, yet commonplace, objects which are washed ...... and left ...... the tide. (CP27) (*n*) The party began shortly ...... nine. Mr Wood, who lived ...... the flat ......, sighed ...... himself as he heard the first signs: the steady tramp ...... feet ...... the stairs; the sound ...... excited voices as the guests greeted one another; and the noise ...... the gramophone, which was turned full ...... Luckily Mr Wood had brought some work home ...... the office, ... which he occupied himself ...... a couple ...... hours, thus managing to ignore ...... some success the party which was going .... his head. But ...... eleven o'clock he felt tired and was ready to go ...... bed, though ...... his experience ...... previous parties he knew that it was useless trying to get to sleep.   (*CP29*)

(*o*) Mr Price got .... bed and went .... the window. The fog had cleared slightly. He opened the window and looked ...... He could just make ...... the shadowy figure ...... a man standing ...... the pavement ...... "What do you want?" Mr Price called .... a nervous voice. The figure stepped ...... until it was standing ...... the streetlamp. It was a policeman. "Sorry to disturb you, sir," said the policeman, "but there is a light .... your shop. I think you have forgotten to turn it ......"   (*CP30*)

Linking Words

Complete each of the following passages by supplying the correct linking word.

(*a*) Our meal was soon over. I tried to go to sleep at once ...... John, ... was a poor sleeper, got out of the car after a few minutes ...... went for a walk up the hill. Soon he came running back. From the top of the hill he had seen, in the valley below, the lights of the town we were looking for. We at once unloaded all our luggage ......, with a great effort, managed to push the car to the top of the hill. ...... we went back for the luggage, loaded the car again ...... set off down the hill. In less than quarter of an hour we were in the town, ... we found a hotel quite easily. (*CP1*)

(*b*) Dawn was just breaking ...... they climbed into their boat ...... pushed off from the bank. A swift current carried them downstream, ... there was no need to row. They took it in turns to keep the boat in the centre of the river. Three hours later they entered the forest ...... they intended to spend the next few days.

"Let's go ashore ...... make some tea," suggested Charles. "No one will see us here."

It was forbidden to light fires in the forest, ... people rarely came this way.

...... Charles tied the boat up, the other two boys set about gathering wood for a fire. ...... they came back, each with a large handful of sticks, they found Charles looking very worried. (*CP4*)

(*c*) ...... Bill entered the gate of Mrs Dunley's house, he was surprised not to find her working in her garden. She usually spent most afternoons there ...... the weather was fine. Bill went straight round to the back of the house, thinking ...... she might be in the kitchen. The door was locked ...... the curtains were drawn. Puzzled, he returned to the front of the house ...... knocked on the door. There was no answer. Bill thought ...... this was very strange ...... he knew ...... Mrs Dunley rarely left the house. (*CP6*)

(*d*) Shortly after the war, my brother and I were invited to spend a few days' holiday with an uncle ...... had just returned from abroad. He had rented a cottage in the country, ... he rarely spent much time there. We understood the reason for this after our arrival: the cottage had no comfortable furniture in it, many of the windows were broken ...... the roof leaked, making the whole house damp.

On our first evening, we sat around the fire after supper listening to the stories ...... our uncle had to tell of his many adventures in distant countries. I was so tired after the long train journey ...... I would have preferred to go to bed; ...... I could not bear to miss any of my uncle's exciting tales. (*CP10*)

(*e*) ...... the train approached the seaside town ...... I was going to spend my holidays, I went into the corridor to stretch my legs. I stayed there for a short while, breathing in the fresh sea air ...... exchanging a few words with one of the passengers, ... I had met earlier on the station platform.

...... I turned to go back to my seat, I happened to glance into the compartment next to mine. Sitting there was a man ...... many years before had been my neighbour. He was a great talker, I remembered; it used to take hours to get away from him ...... he began a conversation. I was not at all sorry ...... he went to live in another part of London. We had not met since then, ... did I wish to meet him now, ... my holiday was about to begin. (*CP12*)

(*f*) ...... at last she reached the door marked "*J. King, Manager*", she knocked rather nervously ...... waited. There was no answer. She tapped on the door again, ... there was still no reply. From inside the next office she could hear the sound of voices, ... she opened the door ...... went in.

...... it was without doubt the same office she had been shown into ...... she had come for an interview with Mr King two weeks before, on that morning it looked quite different. In fact it hardly looked like an office at all. All the employees were standing about, chatting ...... smoking. At the far end of the room a man must have just told a very funny story, ... there was a loud burst of laughter just ...... Mary came in. For a moment she thought ...... they were laughing at her.
(*CP14*)

(*g*) At last, ... what seemed to us an age, the lifeboat reached the man ...... two of the sailors pulled him on board. This was not at all easy, ... the sea was rather rough. ...... the sailors began to row back to the ship again. The lifeboat was raised out of the water ...... the rescued man, wrapped in a blanket, was helped out on to the deck. Leaning on the arm of the ship's doctor, ... still able to walk in spite of his terrible experience, he was led off to the ship's hospital. ...... he passed along the deck everyone cheered wildly. (*CP19*)

(*h*) One summer evening I was sitting by the open window, reading a good but rather frightening mystery story. After a time it became too dark for me to read easily, ... I put my book down ...... got up to switch on the light. I was just about to draw the curtains as well ...... I heard a loud cry of "Help! Help!" It seemed to come from the trees at the end of the garden. I looked out ...... it was now too dark to see any-thing clearly. Almost immediately I heard the cry again. It sounded like a child ...... I could not imagine how anyone could need help in our garden, ... one of the boys of the neigbourhood had climbed a tree ...... could not get down. (*CP21*)

(*i*) ...... I got to the airport, I learnt ...... the plane from Cairo on ...... my brother was travelling, had been delayed in Paris with engine trouble ......was expected to be about an hour late. As a rule I can pass the time quite happily, watching the planes land and take off, ... that evening I had a headache, ... I thought ...... the noise of the engines might make worse. I decided, ..., to walk around to make the time pass quickly.

First of all I went back to the place ...... I had left my car to make sure ...... all the doors were locked. The walk in the fresh air did me good, ... I felt slightly better ...... I entered the main airport building again. I made my way to the restaurant, ... I ordered a cup of black coffee. (*CP25*)

(*j*) The afternoon passed quickly ...... the sun was already beginning to go down ...... the two boys reluctantly decided to turn back ...... make their way homewards. Long ...... they reached the headland, ..., they could see ...... the tide had come in so far ...... they were now cut off from the other part of the beach. They looked at each other in dismay. It was useless to go on, ... clearly there was no way of getting beyond the headland. ......, on the other hand, they went back the way they had just come, the tide would come in long ...... they reached the end of the beach. Their only chance of escape was to find a way up the cliff, ... in some places was not very steep. At least they might be able to climb high enough to be out of reach of the waves, ... were coming closer all the time. (*CP27*)

Section three
Aural Comprehension Tests

Aural Comprehension Passages

(*a*)

Last year three friends of mine decided to spend a holiday in the mountains. They set off by car early in the morning and by the late afternoon they had almost reached the village where they were going to stay. After stopping for a quick cup of tea at a wayside café, they set off again along the winding road that led to the mountains. They had a map with them and according to this the village they were going to stay in was only about fifteen miles away.

It got dark not long after this, and it began to rain too, which of course made it more difficult to see the road clearly. After they had driven for about fifteen miles, there was still no sign of the village. Obviously the map they had was not a very good one.

They went on for another five miles and then the car suddenly stopped. At first my friend thought that they had run out of petrol but, on examination, they found that this was not the trouble. Something else was wrong with the car. Since they could not start the car again, they decided to spend the night in the car, though they had very little food with them and there was not much room for three people.

Early in the morning, a car came along the road. They stopped the driver and asked him where the village was. He told them that it was just on the other side of the hill. They tied their car to his and he pulled them to the top of the hill. After that their car ran all the way downhill to the village, where they found a hotel and had a good breakfast. Of course, if they had walked up the hill the night before, they would not have had to spend an uncomfortable night in the car. (*After CP1*)

1 *Say whether the following statements are true or false.*
 a They drove all day without stopping until the car broke down.
 b They forgot to take a map with them.
 c Their car did not stop because they had run out of petrol.
 d They spent a comfortable night in the car.
 e They had to push their car to the top of the hill.

2 *Answer the following questions.*
 a Where were they going to spend their holiday?

109

b Why was it difficult to see the road?

c What did they ask the driver of the passing car?

d What did the driver tell them?

e What was the first thing they did when they reached the village?

(b)

One cold winter afternoon, the postman was slowly pushing his bicycle up the hill that led out of the village. He was walking very carefully because there was a lot of ice on the ground. He had only one more letter to deliver: this was for an old lady who lived at the top of the hill. Everyone called her "'grandmother". She had lived alone ever since her daughter had emigrated to Australia many years before. She always used to invite the postman in for a cup of tea whenever he took her a letter and tell him about her two grandchildren in Australia, whom she had never seen. Of course she had lots of photographs of them, which she used to show him.

Just as the postman approached her gate, a small boy came running down the hill. Suddenly the boy slipped on the icy road and fell. The postman let his bicycle fall and hurried across the road to help the boy. After a quick examination, he found that the boy had hurt his leg very badly. In fact he thought that the boy's leg might be broken. He knew that "grandmother" did not have a telephone, so he stopped a passing motorist and asked him to take the boy to Dr Stone, who lived in the village. Dr Stone had just retired, after returning from a voyage round the world, but he looked after the boy until they could get an ambulance to take him to hospital. (*After CP6*)

1 *Say whether the following statements are true or false.*

 a The postman had almost finished his day's work.

 b "Grandmother's" daughter was on holiday in Australia.

 c Her grandchildren often used to come to see her.

 d The postman soon found out that the boy had hurt his leg.

 e Dr Stone had never been abroad.

2 *Answer the following questions.*

 a Why was the postman walking up the hill carefully?

 b Where did "grandmother" live?

 c How many grandchildren did she have?

 d What did the postman do when the boy fell?

 e Why did the postman stop a passing motorist?

(c)

Shortly after the war, a friend of mine returned to England after working abroad for most of his life as a doctor. He decided to retire to the country, where he bought himself a small cottage. The cottage was in quite good condition, except for the roof, which leaked rather badly when it rained hard. But my friend, who had led an adventurous life, did not seem to mind that.

Not so long after he had moved in, one of his nephews came down to visit him, without even sending a letter to warn him that he was coming. As his nephew's car drew up outside his gate, my friend saw it from the kitchen window, and for a moment he wondered if he should pretend to be out. He had a good idea what his nephew wanted: he was going to try to borrow some money.

In spite of the fact that the cottage was not very comfortable, my friend's nephew decided to stay for two or three days. As they sat round the fire after supper, my friend told his nephew about some of the exciting adventures he had had abroad. He was just in the middle of one of his stories when there was a tremendous crash upstairs. They both rushed up to the bedroom, where a strange sight met their eyes: part of the ceiling had collapsed, falling right on to the bed where the young man was going to sleep.

After that my friend's nephew did not even want to stay the night, but his uncle persuaded him that it was quite safe to sleep downstairs. The young man went back to London in the morning, however, saying that he had to visit a sick relative.   (After CP10)

1 *Say whether the following statements are true or false.*
   a There was nothing wrong with the cottage except that the roof leaked.
   b The writer's friend knew that his nephew was coming to visit him.
   c He knew that his nephew wanted to borrow money.
   d They did not go to bed immediately after supper.
   e The nephew enjoyed having exciting adventures!

2 *Answer the following questions.*
   a What was the writer's friend doing before he returned to England?
   b Where was he when he saw his nephew's car draw up?
   c What was he doing when they heard the tremendous crash?
   d What did they discover when they opened the bedroom door?
   e What excuse did the young man make for going back to London

the next morning?

(*d*)

One day Mr and Mrs Brown went up to London to do some shopping. They had a busy day, though in the end they did not buy very much, and by about four o'clock they were both looking forward to having a cup of tea. They found a restaurant but, just before they went in, Mrs Brown remembered that she had to buy some medicine for their son, who had a bad cough.

While she was in the chemist's, her husband noticed a bookshop on the other side of the street. He went across to have a look in the window and saw a copy of a novel written by an author who was famous in the last century. He had always been especially interested in this writer, so he went in and bought the book. His wife was waiting for him when he came out. He showed her the book, but she did not look at all pleased: she always used to say that the old books he bought made her house look dirty.

After they had had their cup of tea, they caught the train back to the seaside town where they lived. Much to their surprise, an ex-neighbour of theirs, whom they had not seen for years, got into the same compartment. They were both pleased to see him, after all these years, but, as they soon remembered, he was a great talker. If he got the opportunity, he would talk for hours. However, he happened to notice the book which Mr Brown had bought and he picked it up to examine the title. He opened the book and as he did so, his eyes lit up. He asked Mr Brown how much he had paid for it. Mrs Brown told him: only a few shillings. The man said he was very lucky: the book was a rare edition and was worth several pounds. (*After CP13*)

1 *Say whether the following statements are true or false.*
   a Mr and Mrs Brown bought a lot of things in London.
   b Mrs Brown did not like her husband to buy old books.
   c They got into the same compartment as an ex-neighbour.
   d Mr Brown showed his ex-neighbour the book he had bought.
   e The book was worth much more than Mr Brown had paid for it.

2 *Answer the following questions.*
   a Why did Mrs Brown go to the chemist's?
   b What did Mr Brown do while his wife was at the chemist's?
   c Why didn't Mrs Brown like old books?
   d What did they remember about their ex-neighbour?

e Why did the ex-neighbour say that Mr Brown was lucky?

(*e*)

It was Monday morning. Edna left home early that day because she was going to start work at an office in the city. She was only sixteen and this was her first job. There were a lot of people at the bus-stop and she nearly took a taxi which was passing; but afterwards she was glad that she waited for the bus. The traffic was so dense that even if she had taken a taxi, she would not have arrived much earlier. As it was, she was only a few minutes late.

She caught the lift up to the eighth floor and went along to the office where she had been interviewed by Mr Crump two weeks before. This was the man she was going to work for. She tapped on the door and waited, but there was no reply. Just then she heard the sound of someone's voice from the next office. She opened the door and looked in. There was Mr Crump, speaking to the people in the office in an angry voice. Then he turned round and left the room.

Later in the day, Edna found out what had happened. Apparently Mr Crump came to the office as a rule about nine-thirty, because he lived a long way out in the country and came up by train every day. That morning, however, he happened to catch an earlier train, and when he arrived in the office, not a single person was working. They were all standing around, smoking, chatting and telling jokes.

1 *Say whether the following statements are true or false.*
   a Edna had to take a taxi to the office.
   b There was a lot of traffic that morning.
   c There was somebody in Mr Crump's office.
   d Mr Crump did not live in London.
   e Mr Crump had arrived early that morning.

2 *Answer the following questions.*
   a Why was Edna glad that she did not take a taxi?
   b Who was Mr Crump?
   c Why did Edna open the door of the next office?
   d What time did Mr Crump usually arrive?
   e What did Mr Crump see when he arrived that morning?

(*f*)

I went to a meeting of our Literary Society last night. We had a most interesting speaker, a man by the name of Weston, who has written several books. He is in fact the person who was invited to address the society on the occasion of our fifth anniversary, but unfortunately he was ill at the time. He had been overworking and as a result his doctor ordered him to take a complete rest for at least three months.

However, he was recovered from his illness now and last night he told us about his most recent work. It is a book about the famous traveller, Colonel Manning, who lived in India in the early part of this century. Weston said that for years he had been planning to write a book about Colonel Manning but, apart from a collection of letters and notes which the family had provided him with, he did not have much material.

Then one day he got a letter from one of Colonel Manning's nephews, saying that his uncle had kept a diary. Weston at once went round to see Manning's daughter to enquire about them. She was not aware that her father had kept a diary but she suggested that he should look in the attic, where some of his boxes were stored. One of these was locked, but Miss Manning managed, after searching through a number of drawers, to find the right key. When they opened the box, Weston was delighted to find a bundle of exercise books inside. They were the diaries he was looking for, and with the help of these he was able to write a very full account of Colonel Manning's life.   (*After CP16*)

1 *Say whether the following statements are true or false.*
  a Weston was not able to address the Literary Society on the occasion of its fifth anniversary.
  b Weston had been ill because he worked too hard.
  c Colonel Manning's family had given Weston enough material to write an account of their father's life.
  d Colonel Manning's daughter knew where her father's diaries were.
  e It took Colonel Manning's daughter a little time to find the key to the box.

2 *Answer the following questions.*
  a Why wasn't Weston able to address the Literary Society on the occasion of their fifth anniversary?
  b Who was Colonel Manning?
  c How did Weston come to hear about Colonel Manning's diaries?
  d What did they find inside the locked box?
  e How did the diaries help Weston?
(*g*)
For three days Inspector Robinson had been completely in the dark. A man had been found unconscious in the car park of the Swan Hotel. He had been robbed and his car had been stolen. The police had no idea of his identity until at last the man was able to tell them who he was and

what had happened. He was also able to give them a description of the man, which the police sent to all the newspapers.

The next day Inspector Robinson got a message to say that the man had been seen in a small seaside town. Inspector Robinson immediately went there. When he reached the police-station, the inspector in charge had a second message for him. The owner of a small restaurant on the seafront had just telephoned. According to him, a person like the wanted man was having dinner in his restaurant.

The police at once rushed round to the restaurant. Two policemen stayed outside the front entrance, while Inspector Robinson and another man entered through the kitchen. Very excited, the owner of the restaurant showed Inspector Robinson the man he had been watching. He was sitting at a corner table, reading a newspaper. Without doubt it was the right man.

Inspector Robinson did not want to disturb the other people in the restaurant. He let the man finish his meal. Then, as he left the restaurant, Inspector Robinson followed him into the street and arrested him.

1 *Say whether the following statements are true or false.*
   a The police had no idea at first who the unconscious man was.
   b The wanted man was soon seen.
   c All the four policemen went into the restaurant.
   d Inspector Robinson had a look at the man before he arrested him.
   e Inspector Robinson arrested the man in the restaurant.

2 *Answer the following questions.*
   a What had happened to the man in the car park?
   b How was the injured man able to help the police?
   c Why did the owner of the restaurant telephone the police?
   d What was the wanted man doing when Inspector Robinson saw him?
   e Why did Inspector Robinson let the man finish his meal?

(*h*)
It is a strange experience coming back to the place where you were born and brought up, after an absence of several years. This happened to me a few months ago when I decided to return to Dunley to take up the post of chief reporter on a newspaper there.

I got the job through the father of an old schoolfriend of mine. I met him at his son's wedding and when I finally decided to go back to Dunley, principally because I was tired of living in London, I wrote to him in the hope that he might be able to put me in touch with people. By a strange coincidence he knew that the editor of the newspaper wanted a reporter. As it turned out, I was just the right person because I had had wide experience and at the same time I knew Dunley.

In a way, however, this was not true. I quickly discovered that I did not know the town at all well when I came to look for somewhere to live. Many parts of it had completely changed. Having to look for a flat helped me to rediscover it, for I had to search hard before I found what I wanted.

In the end I got the right sort of place: a flat in a large house in a very quiet street. It looked on to the park and I felt at once that this was just the place for me. Moreover, the rent was very moderate, so I took the flat without any hesitation. *(After CP23)*

1 *Say whether the following statements are true or false.*

　a The writer had not lived in Dunley for quite a long time.
　b He went back to work for the father of a schoolfriend.
　c He found that he still knew Dunley well.
　d It was not easy for him to find somewhere to live.
　e The flat he found was expensive.

2 *Answer the following questions.*

　a What job did the writer take up when he went back to Dunley?
　b Where did he meet his friend's father?
　c Why was he the right person for the job?
　d How did he get to know Dunley again?
　e What were the things that he liked about the flat?

(i)

When Tom decided to go on a holiday to England, he wrote to a friend of his who was living in London and asked if he could meet him at the airport. The friend wrote back to say that he would be there. So Tom was rather surprised when he reached the airport to find that his friend had not turned up.

He walked around for a short while and then, because he had a slight headache, went into the restaurant and had a cup of strong, black coffee. After that he felt much better. He bought a couple of magazines at the bookstall and went into the lounge to read them. He felt sure that his friend would come fairly soon, though he was beginning to get worried.

He had just started to read his magazine when his friend arrived, with a young lady. Tom's friend apologised for being late and explained what had happened. Apparently he had arranged to meet the young lady at six o'clock, just outside the underground station not far from where he was living. The young lady, who had only travelled on the underground once before, had set out in good time but unfortunately she had got on a train going in the wrong direction. She travelled for several stops before she realised this, because the train was very crowded and she could not see the names of the stations. By the time she got to the right station, she was nearly three-quarters of an hour late. (*After CP25*)

1 *Say whether the following statements are true or false.*
    a Tom expected to find his friend waiting at the airport.
    b He went to look for his friend in the restaurant.
    c He went back to the restaurant to read his magazines.
    d Tom's friend lived near the underground station.
    e If the train had not been crowded, the young lady would have been able to see the names of the stations.

2 *Answer the following questions.*
    a Why did Tom write to his friend?
    b Why did he want a cup of black coffee?
    c What did Tom's friend do when he arrived?
    d Why was the young lady late?
    e At what time did the young lady reach the right station?

(*j*)
Henry's interview ought to have begun at eleven, but the librarian was on the phone when Henry was shown into his office. Henry sat down in one of the armchairs near the window and waited. It sounded as if this was a long distance call, because at times the librarian was having to shout to make himself heard, and he was beginning to get rather impatient.

Henry had come about a job in the reference library, for which he had seen an advertisement in the paper. At present he was working as a clerk in the accounts section of a big office, and he did not enjoy the work at all. He rather liked the idea of having a job in the reference library. He used to spend quite a lot of time there in the evenings, studying especially the books on photography, which was one of his hobbies.

While he was waiting for the librarian to finish his long distance call, Henry picked up one of the new books which were lying on a coffee table at his side. It was a book of adventure stories for boys. Henry began to read one of them—a story about two boys who were cut off by the tide after spending the day on a deserted beach, and he had almost finished it by the time the librarian was ready to begin the interview.

(*After CP27*)

1 *Say whether the following statements are true or false.*
   a Henry's interview began punctually at eleven.
   b The librarian had to shout while he was speaking on the phone because there was a lot of noise outside.
   c Henry liked his present job.
   d He knew the reference library quite well already.
   e He sat and listened to the librarian's telephone conversation all the time.

2 *Answer the following questions.*
   a Why did Henry have to wait?
   b Why had Henry come to see the librarian?
   c How did he hear about the job in the reference library?
   d Where was Henry working at present?
   e What was the story which he read about?

Dictation Passages

(*a*)

Of the four other people at our table, / two were men / and two were women. / One of the men was a doctor, / travelling round the world for the last time, / before he retired to a quiet country village. / The other man was an engineer, / with such a loud laugh / that I could hear it in my cabin, / which was next to his. / One of the women was a grandmother, / though she looked remarkably young, / She was on her way / to visit her daughter, / who had emigrated to Australia / several years before. / The other woman was going / to join her husband in India. / She only spoke / when she wanted to consult the doctor / about her children's ailments. (*After CP3*)

(*b*)

First of all I waded downstream / to the place where our boat was hidden / in the shelter of some overhanging bushes. / I then rowed the boat back / to the old bridge, / where the water was shallow. / and we loaded it / with the provisions for the expedition. / It took about half an hour. / Dawn was just breaking / as we set off down the river. / When we reached the forest / three hours later, / we decided to go ashore / to make some tea. / I tied the boat up, / while the other boys gathered wood. / Unluckily, / although they found plenty of sticks, / we could not light a fire after all, / because we had forgotten to bring any matches./ (*After CP4*)

(*c*)

A young lady was waiting at the bus-stop / with her small suitcase beside her / on the pavement. / She kept glancing anxiously / at her watch. / Her train left at two-thirty / and it was already ten past two. / She did not want to miss her train, / so she decided to telephone for a taxi, / although the fare to the station / was more than she could afford. / She had already walked some distance / in the direction of a friend's house, / where there was a telephone, / when a bus came into sight. / She ran back at once / towards the bus-stop, / and managed to catch the bus, / which had stopped / to let some passengers get off. (*After CP7*)

(*d*)

One day when I got home, / tired after a morning's shopping, / I found I had lost my purse. / I at once retraced my steps / as far as the chemist's in the main road, / where I had bought some medicine, / but there was no sign of the purse / on the pavement. / Luckily, / there was not much money in it, / only some small change; / but it also contained / a photograph of my daughter, / taken when she was twelve years old, / which

I was very fond of / and always carried with me. / Later in the day, / I called at the police station / to enquire if the purse had been found. / I was pleased to learn / that someone had handed it in. / The sergeant had made a note / of the man's name and address, / so I was able to write / and thank him. *(After CP11)*

(e)
I went last summer / to spend my holidays at the seaside. / Just before the train reached the station, / I took my suitcases / out of the compartment / and carried them / to the end of the corridor. / After I had done this, / I stood by the open window, / breathing in the fresh sea air. / Imagine my surprise / when a familiar voice greeted me. / It was my neighbour! / He was not only going for his holiday / to the same seaside town, / but also, / as I soon discovered, / had chosen the same hotel / to stay in. / It was a remarkable coincidence. *(After CP12)*

(f)
In our grandfather's house, / there was an attic, / the door to which was always kept locked. / One day, / however, / my sister found the key in a drawer, / so with great excitement / we set off up the stairs / to explore the locked room. / When we managed to open the door / we could see nothing at first. / Then I noticed a small window, / high up in the roof. / It was dirty, / so that hardly any light came through. / I climbed on to a box / and pushed it open, / thus letting in more light. / But we found nothing of interest; / even the large box / which was I standing on / contained only old papers. *(After CP15)*

(g)
As I was walking along the road / the other day / my curiosity was aroused / by a small crowd which had gathered / around the entrance to the park. / On crossing the road, / I discovered that the centre of attraction / was an old man / with a performing monkey. / The monkey's tricks / were quite remarkable, / so that in a short time / the hat which the old man had placed on the pavement / was half filled with coins, / many of them silver. / It seemed to me an easy way / of making a good living. *(After CP17)*

(h)
As soon as the ship began to turn round, / most of the passengers / left the dining-room / and rushed up on deck. / There they found / that a lifeboat had been lowered / into the sea. / An officer shouted an order / to the four sailors sitting at the oars / and they began to row / in the direction of the man / who had been seen / floating in the sea. / After what seemed an age, / they reached the man, / pulled him on board, / and rowed back to the ship. / The lifeboat was raised out of the water, / and the rescued man, / wrapped only in a blanket, / was carried to the

ship's hospital.   (*After CP19*)
(*i*)
The cry seemed to come from the trees / at the far end of my garden. /
I stood by the window / and listened. / Again I heard the cry. / It sounded
/ as if someone was in trouble, / so I decided to go out / and have a look
in the garden. / Since it was getting dark, / I took the torch / which we
keep for going into the cellar, / where there is no electric light, / and
with the help of this, / I examined the far end of the garden / and the
lower branches of the trees. / But there was no sign of anybody. / In the
end, / I came to the conclusion / that one of the boys / who lived in the
neighbourhood / was playing a joke on me.   (*After CP21*)
(*j*)
As Peter glanced down the newspaper / which he had bought from the
station bookstall, / a notice in bold capital letters / caught his eye. / It
gave the name and address / of an accommodation agency / which had
flats and rooms to let. / After breakfast, / therefore, / he set out in search /
of the agency. / He found it, / without much difficulty, / in a narrow
street / just off the main road. / He explained to the woman at the desk /
exactly what kind of room he wanted, / and for the small fee of five
shillings / she gave him a list / of about half a dozen landladies / who had
rooms to let.   (*After CP23*)
(*k*)
I shall never forget the first time / I travelled by tube / in London. / I
had to wait in a long queue / to get my ticket, / and when at last my turn
came, / I had some difficulty / in pronouncing the name of the station /
which I wanted to go to. / I got the right ticket in the end, / however, /
and I also managed to find the right platform, / though I had to ask
several people the way. The tram train emerged from the tunnel with a
terrifying roar, / and I was swept on to the train / by people pushing
from behind. / The train moved off / before I could get my breath back. /
It was packed tight with people / and I could not even see the names of
the stations / where we stopped. / Luckily, / I had counted the number
of stops, / so I knew exactly / where to get off.   (*After CP24*)
(*l*)
After lunch, / the two boys set off along the beach / which lay beyond
the headland. / It was like discovering a new world. / They explored
innumerable caves, / half expecting in each / to come across smugglers
there. / They looked for fish / and other sea-creatures / in the small
pools among the rocks. / They examined all the objects / which had been
washed up by the tide / and lay upon the beach. / In this way / the afternoon passed quickly, / and the sun was already beginning to set / as they
reluctantly decided / to make their way homewards.   (*After CP27*)

Reading goals for each passage

1 Which title is better? *An adventure in the hills* or *A night on the road*
2 How did the photo help the writer to find the owner of the purse?
3 Who are the four other people at the table? Where are they going to?
4 What was the 'bad' news?
5 Which boy was absent? Where was he? Why?
6 How did Bill get into Mrs Dunley's house?
7 How did Helen travel to the station?
8 How did Mrs Cross help Mr White?
9 Edna is going to meet Rosemary. Where? When? Why?
10 Which title is better? *A terrifying adventure* or *A lucky escape*
11 Two people helped Mrs Brown. Who were they? How did they help her?
12 Which title is better? *A pleasant surprise!* or *No escape!* or *A perfect holiday!*
13 Fred took some old books to a bookseller. Why? Was he pleased?
14 What were people in the office doing: a) at 9.15   b) at 9.45
15 What was West looking for? Did he find them?
16 Who is J.N. Edwards? Who did he write to? Who answered his letter? Why?
17 Which title is better? *How to kill a monkey* or *How to make money out of a monkey*
18 Give these details about the interview: People ... Place ... Purpose ...
19 Which title is better? *A rescue at sea* or *A storm at sea* or *An accident at sea*
20 Which title is better? *The wrong place* or *The wrong time* or *The wrong man*
21 The writer heard a cry for help in the garden. Was someone playing a joke on him?
22 Who is John Smith? What is his problem? Can Bill Ratcliffe help him?
23 What was Peter looking for? How many houses did he go to?
24 Which of these things did Tom do? a) He went to the wrong platform
    b) He got on the wrong train   c) He got the wrong ticket
25 Which of these did the writer buy at the airport? a) coffee   b) ticket
    c) newspaper   d) magazines
26 How did Phillip disturb the readers in the Reference Library? Did he have to leave?
27 Why did the boys have to be rescued? Because they were: a) drowning
    b) lost   c) trapped
28 Complete: People ... Place ... Purpose of meeting ...
29 Mr Wood went upstairs a) to complain   b) to get an invitation to the party
30 Was Mr Price afraid a) when the doorbell rang   b) when he opened the door?